THE MEXICAN-AMERICAN WAR

CHRONICLE OF AMERICA'S WARS

Ruth Tenzer Feldman

LERNER PUBLICATIONS COMPANY

MINNEAPOLIS

CHAPTER PHOTO CAPTIONS

Introduction: Mexican and U.S. troops clash at the Battle of Cerro Gordo in April 1847.

Chapter 1: An early map of North America shows Mexican and U.S. territories before the Mexican-American War.

Chapter 2: Wagon trains crisscross the country as settlers move into the western territories of the United States.

Chapter 3: Zachary "Old Rough and Ready" Taylor, nicknamed for his relaxed leadership style, commanded U.S. troops against Mexico's army in the Mexican-American War.

Chapter 4: In the summer of 1846, John Frémont and his battalion of frontiersmen marched to Monterey and enlisted in the U.S. Army. The army took control of northern California, angering the Mexicans who lived there.

Chapter 5: The city of Chihuahua, as seen from the cathedral, lies in the high desert of central Mexico.

Chapter 6: U.S. soldiers fight their way up a steep hill to attack the Mexican position in the Battle of Cerro Gordo in April 1847.

Chapter 7: Mayor General John Quitman and his troops enter Mexico City after the United States defeated Mexico in the Mexican-American War.

Chapter 8: The signing of the Gadsden Purchase Treaty on July 4, 1854, gave the United States an additional 29,640 square miles of territory that had once belonged to Mexico.

Lerner Publications Company
A division of Lerner Publishing Group
241 First Avenue North
Minneapolis, MN 55401

Website address: www.lernerbooks.com

Library of Congress Cataloging-in-Publication Data

Feldman, Ruth Tenzer.
  The Mexican-American War / by Ruth Tenzer Feldman.
    p. cm. — (Chronicle of America's wars)
  Includes bibliographical references (p. 85) and index.
    Contents: Bordering on war — Manifest destiny — Rough and ready — Continuing conflict —
Conquering peace — March to Mexico City — The struggle for peace — Two nations, one border.
  ISBN 0–8225–0831–1 (lib. bdg. : alk. paper)
    1. Mexican War, 1846–1848—Juvenile literature. [1. Mexican War, 1846–1848.] I. Title. II. Series.
E404.F45 2004
973.6'2—dc22   2003023395

Manufactured in the United States of America
1 2 3 4 5 6 – JR – 09 08 07 06 05 04

TABLE OF CONTENTS

INTRODUCTION

April 15, 1847. It was hot in central Mexico. Food supplies for U.S. Army troops were running low. Disease was running high. Many men who had volunteered to serve in the war against Mexico had nearly finished their one-year tour of duty and were eager to go home. They had captured the port of Veracruz along the Gulf of Mexico and marched about 50 miles through swampy lowlands toward the mountain plateau surrounding Mexico City, the capital of Mexico, their final target.

By April 13, they were stuck. Mexican military commander Antonio López de Santa Anna was determined to stop U.S. forces at Cerro Gordo, the first high hill after the swamps and coastal plains. He had assembeled a large defensive line of men and artillery (large, mounted firearms) across the one road that U.S. troops could take to advance toward Mexico City. General Winfield Scott, who commanded U.S. forces, decided that a direct attack against Mexican forces would result in great losses and possible defeat. Retreat was unacceptable to him.

On April 15, Scott ordered Robert E. Lee, a captain in the engineering corps, to slip behind enemy lines to look for a weak link in Mexican defenses. Now Captain Lee was also stuck.

Scouting near a spring, Lee heard voices speaking Spanish. He scrambled under a

fallen tree just as Mexican soldiers came out of the nearby brush to drink at the spring. They left, and other Mexican soldiers came. Hour after hour, Lee lay motionless. Insects stung and bit him. The heat made him dizzy with thirst. Mexican soldiers climbed over the fallen tree to drink at the spring or sat and rested on it, inches from his face.

It had been 18 years since Captain Lee graduated with honors from the United States Military Academy at West Point in New York. He was 40 years old, with a wife and seven children in Virginia. Lee was an ace in topography (mapping) and an expert engineer. He had helped to build or repair several military forts and had designed harbor facilities at St.

Louis, Missouri. But Captain Lee had never before been in battle.

As dusk fell, he crawled away from his fallen tree hideout and returned to base. The next morning, he was back again, at the same area, determined to discover the best way for U.S. troops to advance. As he had written to his wife earlier, "I am one of those . . . persons when I have any thing to do I can't rest satisfied until it has been accomplished."

Lee would play a major role in the war between Mexico and the United States—a conflict known as the Mexican-American War, which would give the United States vast lands in the Southwest and West and establish the border between these two great nations.

BORDERING ON WAR

When Antonio López de Santa Anna first entered the army, Mexico was a colony of Spain. When Mexico rebelled against Spain, Santa Anna first fought on Spain's side, then for Mexico. Mexico gained its independence in 1821. The new nation claimed all North American territory that had been under Spanish control—including all of California and Texas, and most of the land in between.

In 1821 the United States and newly independent Mexico were about equal in size. After independence from Britain, the new United States governed a relatively small strip of land along the Atlantic Coast. But Mexico had a vast territory to govern and little experience with which to govern it. Mexico also lost about 10 percent of its young men during its war for independence from Spain, and the country was left with an enormous debt.

Mexico's first leader was Augustín de Iturbide. When he declared himself emperor, leaders from different regions of Mexico rose up to seek their independence from the central government in Mexico City. In 1822 Santa Anna declared the area around the city of Veracruz a separate republic. When Iturbide's army nearly crushed Santa Anna's rebellion, leaders of other provinces (states) came to his defense.

Iturbide gave up power in 1823. The Mexican Congress approved a constitution in 1824, but political reform and democratic elections were slow in coming. Some states and cities had their own militia (soldiers called to serve in an emergency), and their leaders wanted a weak central government. Riots broke out in Mexico City between rival groups about giving the poor the right to vote. At the same time, the economy was devastated and Mexican money was almost worthless.

During this chaotic time, rumors spread that Mexico contained gold and other natural resources. Many nations wanted to get those resources and take control of the vast territories that had belonged to Spain. One of these nations was the United States.

Mexico was not interested in selling newly won lands. But it did want to attract immigrants to sparsely settled regions. One of those regions was Texas. In 1821 only about 2,500 Mexicans lived in Texas, most of them living in the provincial capital of San Antonio. The 1824 constitution provided that each state in Mexico should have its own constitution. The state of Coahuila was combined with the less populated province of Texas, and the new capital became Saltillo.

The new governments in Mexico City and Saltillo offered land for farming and cattle raising to immigrants of European background (Anglos) so long as they agreed to become Catholic, the national religion of Mexico. Mexico wanted to increase the population in Texas so that there would be enough people in this region to build an economy and defend Mexico's borders against possible invasion from the United States or other countries. These settlers could also help control the bandits who preyed on inhabitants of the region.

Stephen Austin

Land speculators, known as *empresarios,* bought up thousands of acres and established settlements for English, Irish, German, and other immigrants. Stephen Austin, who inherited land that his father had been given by Mexico, was the first empresario to establish such a settlement.

This illustration pictures Austin, Texas, as it appeared during its settlement in the early 1800s. Stephen Austin brought 300 families to help settle Texas.

Austin Helps Mexico

Texas empresario Stephen Austin met with the Mexican leaders who drafted the Mexican Constitution of 1824, which resembles parts of the Constitution of the United States. Farmers in Austin's colony (settlement) contributed bushels of corn to help pay the expenses of Juan José María Erasmo Seguín, who represented Texas in the first Mexican Congress.

Many of these new Texans governed themselves locally, had little loyalty to Mexico, and did not convert to Catholicism. In 1827 a group of Anglo settlers in Texas tried to form an independent state called the Republic of Fredonia. The rebellion was quickly squashed. After Andrew Jackson became president of the United States in 1828, he offered to buy Texas from Mexico, but Mexico refused. Then in 1829, Spain tried to recapture Mexico. Santa Anna became the commander of Mexico's army and defeated Spain's attempt.

Mexico tried to gain better control of the Texas settlers. In 1830 Mexico prohibited any further immigration to Texas and increased its military presence in the area. But immigrants continued to arrive. By the 1830s, about 35,000 people lived in Texas, mainly from the United States. These settlers felt different from and superior to the native Mexican people in Texas, and they maintained close ties to friends and family in the United States.

A popular military commander, Santa Anna became president of Mexico. Once in power, he angered many Mexicans by

Mexican general Santa Anna *(standing pointing)* led Mexico's army in winning independence from Spain in 1829.

revoking (cancelling) the 1824 constitution. Revolts sprang up in California, New Mexico Territory, the Yucatán, Texas, and elsewhere. A group of Texans also wanted to repeal (overturn) the 1830 law banning immigration. They drafted a proposed constitution for the state of Texas—separate from Coahuila—and Stephen Austin took the constitution to Mexico City along with a list of demands for reform.

Santa Anna refused statehood for Texas and jailed Austin on suspicion of trying to start a revolution. Mexican troops put down the revolts everywhere but in Texas, where a volunteer army of Texans captured San Antonio.

> **EYEWITNESS QUOTE:**
>
> "Texas is Mexico's most valuable possession; I pray God that our neglect will not lead to the loss of such a precious part of our territory."
>
> —Colonel Juan Nepomuceno Almonte, 1834

at the Alamo, a small mission-turned-fort near San Antonio. Santa Anna and about 1,800 soldiers arrived there on February 23, 1836, to retake it.

While fighting went on at the Alamo, a group of American Texans met in Washington-on-the-Brazos, a small town northeast of San Antonio. On March 2, they voted 33 to 15 to declare independence from Mexico and create the Lone Star Republic, an independent country. They named empresario David Burnet acting president and made Sam Houston commander of the armed forces.

THE LONE STAR REPUBLIC

The head of the Texas rebels was Sam Houston, a close friend of President Jackson. Houston led a few hundred men, who were stationed at San Antonio and at the Texas towns of Goliad and Gonzales. Soon after Austin was released from jail in Mexico in 1835, he traveled to Washington, D.C., to seek money and men for the Texas rebellion. Hundreds of volunteers came from the United States to help, including former Tennessee congressman Davy Crockett. Crockett was one of nearly 200 men

Sam Houston

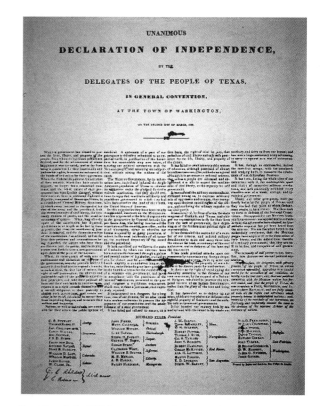

On March 2, 1836, a group of Texans signed the Declaration of Independence from Mexico. But Mexico did not recognize the Texans' wishes.

Texans fought Mexico's army in the famous Battle of the Alamo in 1836.

The Alamo fell to Santa Anna's forces several days later, and all the rebels there were killed. General Houston ordered the 340 men stationed at Goliad to retreat and surrender. A Mexican law stated that non-Mexicans settling in Texas after 1830 were illegal aliens, and all illegal aliens fighting against the Mexican government would be executed as pirates. Santa Anna ordered the surrendering Texans to be shot.

Santa Anna's actions outraged many people in Texas and the United States. The rallying cry for citizens of the new Lone Star Republic was "Remember the Alamo and Goliad!" Houston's remaining men surprised Mexican troops near the San Jacinto River in late April. They slaughtered many of them and captured Santa Anna.

President Jackson persuaded Houston to send Santa Anna with a small escort to Washington, D.C., 1,700 miles away.

While Santa Anna headed for Washington, Stephen Austin was returning to Texas. Citizens of the Lone Star Republic approved a constitution. They elected Sam Houston their president and voted 3,277 to 19 to join the United States. Austin became secretary of state. He died later that year.

In January 1837, U.S. president Jackson greeted Santa Anna with the pomp and ceremony due a head of state. Jackson offered to give aid to Mexico if Mexico recognized the independence of Texas. But Anastasio Bustamante, who was elected Mexico's president in Santa Anna's absence, stated that Santa Anna had no

General Santa Anna *(standing left in white pants)* surrendered to General Sam Houston *(lying on ground)* on April 22, 1836, and signed a treaty giving Texas its independence. But Santa Anna was no longer president, so the treaty was not recognized by the Mexican government.

power to bind Mexico to any agreements. Santa Anna returned to his estate in Mexico near Veracruz.

The United States formally recognized the Lone Star Republic. But it was not clear what the southern border of the new country was. After Mexico gained independence from Spain, most mapmakers in Spain, Europe, and the United States drew the southern border of the province of Texas at the Nueces River. But when Texas declared its independence, it drew the southern border farther south at the Rio Grande, which added more land to the new country. Mexico refused to recognize the Rio Grande border and marched troops into the disputed territory.

Mexico had other troubles besides the Texas rebels. The country was deeply in debt. France demanded that Mexico give France special trading privileges and pay for damage done to the property of French citizens in Mexico during Mexico's war of independence. To back up its demands, France sent ships to blockade (block off) the port of Veracruz, preventing all trade. Then France charged Mexico for the costs of the blockade.

President Bustamante refused to pay France. French warships in Veracruz harbor shelled the city. When French sailors went ashore, Santa Anna rushed on horseback from his nearby estate to defend Veracruz. Just before the French sailors returned to their ships, one of them shot Santa Anna in the leg. The next day, doctors amputated his mangled leg below the knee, and Santa Anna became a national hero.

President Bustamante settled the war with France in 1839, but he was not able to maintain a stable government for Mexico. In 1841 Santa Anna regained the presidency. Mexico refused to recognize the Lone Star Republic. Presidents Santa Anna of Mexico and Houston of the Lone Star Republic continued to challenge each other over the disputed territory between the Nueces River and the Rio Grande. Fighting along the border used up most of the government's money in both Texas and Mexico. Santa Anna imposed heavy taxes on the Mexican people but took huge sums for himself. For example, he had an elaborate funeral for his amputated leg.

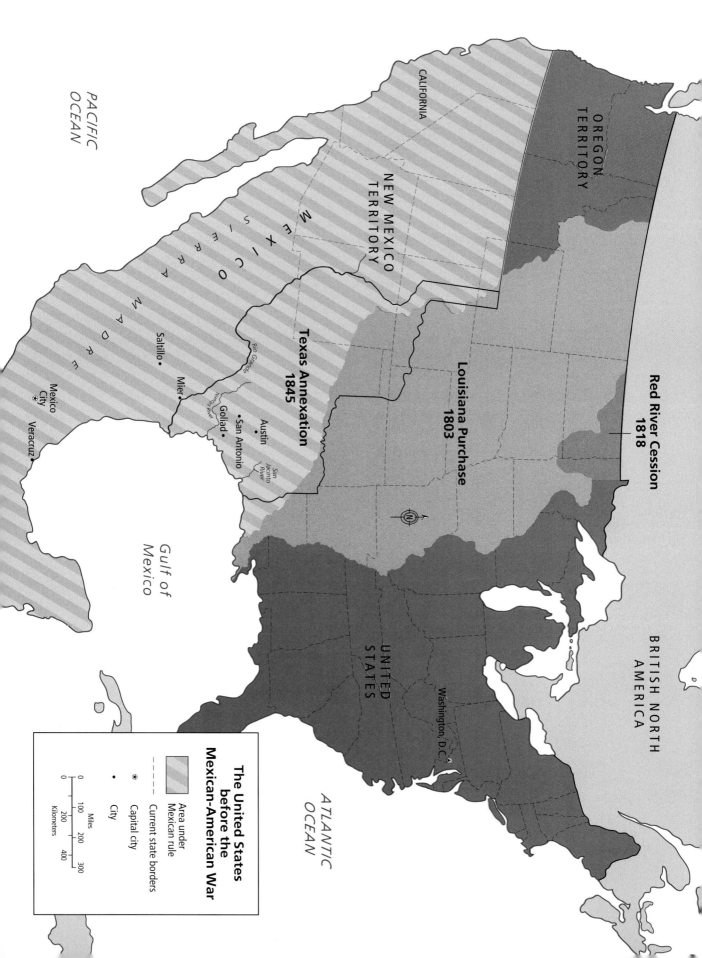

The United States before the
Mexican-American War

Area under
Mexican rule

Current state borders

Capital city

City

Miles
0   100 200 300
0   100 200 300 400
Kilometers

PACIFIC
OCEAN

CALIFORNIA

OREGON
TERRITORY

NEW MEXICO
TERRITORY

M E X I C O

S I E R R A   M A D R E

Saltillo

Mexico
City

Mier

Veracruz

Río Grande

Nueces River

Goliad

San Antonio

Austin

San
Jacinto
River

Texas Annexation
1845

Louisiana Purchase
1803

Red River Cession
1818

Gulf of
Mexico

UNITED
STATES

Washington, D.C.

ATLANTIC
OCEAN

BRITISH NORTH
AMERICA

TYLER'S TRIUMPH

John Tyler, who became U.S. president in April 1841, was determined to make the Lone Star Republic part of the United States. Taking a cue from France's brief war with Mexico, Tyler billed Mexico $2 million for damages against the United States during the Mexican war for independence.

Tyler first had to face the possibility of war with Britain over land in the Pacific Northwest. In the Adams-Onís Treaty of 1819, Spain gave up its right to territory that was north of the border between the Spanish state of California and Oregon Territory. In treaties a few years later, Russia, which had had fur trading posts in California, gave up its claim to territories south of the southern border of Alaska. The United States and Britain argued over who had the right to the vast area in between, including what is present-day Oregon, Washington, and the Canadian province of British Columbia.

Meanwhile, Santa Anna's treatment of rebellious Texans increased the sympathy of people in the United States for their friends and relatives in the new republic, even when Texans caused trouble in Mexican territory. In one incident, about 300 Texans crossed the Rio Grande on December 23, 1842, and entered the Mexican town of Mier. They demanded that the townspeople bring supplies to their camp. Then they took the town's mayor as a hostage. When supplies did not show up, the Texans learned that a group of Mexican soldiers had prevented their delivery.

The Texans attacked Mier, and after a fierce battle with Mexican troops, the surviving Texans surrendered. Mexico exe-

Gold

In 1834 Native Americans brought gold flakes to the mission (a religious establishment that works to spread its faith and to provide humanitarian services to an area) in San Fernando, California. Rumors spread that the mission priests were secretly mining gold. In 1842 a major vein of gold was discovered, when, according to legend, Francisco López pulled wild onions near an oak tree on his Placerita Canyon ranch and found gold nuggets caught in their roots. None of the early discoveries of gold yielded much.

cuted the leader of the group and every tenth man, and imprisoned the rest. Many of them died in captivity. Andrew Jackson got involved, and Santa Anna, remembering Jackson's courteous treatment of him several years earlier, released the remaining men in September 1844.

That same month, Tyler sent Andrew Jackson Donelson to be the U.S. ambassador to the Lone Star Republic. Donelson was the nephew of former president Jackson and knew Sam Houston. His assignment was to report on possibilities for annexation of Texas (joining it to the United States) and, if possible, to stay alive. Four previous ambassadors to the Lone Star Republic had died of a tropical disease called yellow fever soon after they reached their post.

President Tyler also sent Duff Green to Mexico with offers to buy California and New Mexico. When Mexico refused, Green was reassigned to investigate tensions between the Texans and the Mexicans.

Some historians claim that Green was sent to the Lone Star Republic to help start a war.

In the 1844 U.S. presidential campaign, Democrat James Polk supported annexation of Texas. He won the close November elections by a small number of votes. One month later, Santa Anna was driven from office by military commander Mariano Paredes y Arrillaga. He went into exile in Cuba.

José Joaquín Herrera became Mexico's next president. Herrera took the unpopular position that Mexico should recognize Texas as a separate nation so long as Texas did not become a part of the United States. He wanted time to solve Mexico's economic and social problems—and to maintain national pride—without engaging in another war so soon after Mexico's war of independence. But the Mexican Congress would not let Herrera give up Texas, and he failed to form a solid government.

A few days before President Tyler left office in March 1845, the U.S. Congress called for the Lone Star Republic to become part of the United States. The new U.S. president, James Polk, made it clear that annexation was up to the Texans, not Herrera. The United States broke diplomatic relations with Mexico.

On July 4, 1845, Texans voted to join the United States of America. Fearing war, President Polk put the U.S. Navy on alert. He sent the Pacific Squadron of the navy to the coast of California and the Home Squadron to the Gulf of Mexico.

The United States argued that the southern border of the soon-to-be state of Texas was the Rio Grande. But President Polk ordered U.S. soldiers only to the northeastern side of the Nueces River. Mexico argued that the Nueces River was the proper boundary. But President Herrera sent troops only to the southern side of the Rio Grande. The world waited to see which country would step into the disputed land between these two rivers and start a war.

> ### EYEWITNESS QUOTE: WAR OVER TEXAS
>
> **"War with the United States over Texas is a bottomless abyss [hole] into which our Republic will sink along with all our hopes for the future."**
>
> **—José Joaquín Herrera, president of Mexico**

2 MANIFEST DESTINY

"Our age is...of a different character from the past," said Daniel Webster. "Society is full of excitement." Webster was describing the United States in the 1840s. Industry was booming. Samuel Morse's telegraph, invented in 1844, revolutionized communication. There were new railroads, canals, and highways. Art and culture thrived.

Senator Webster had opposed adding Texas to the United States. Texans allowed slavery, and he worried about the political battles that adding another slave state would cause. But others were eager for the United States to grow. Some saw western expansion as a form of national security. More U.S. territory in North America meant less territory for European powers such as Britain and France to colonize (settle).

Some saw western expansion as the United States' god-given right. An article calling for the annexation of Texas in the July–August 1845 issue of the *United States Magazine and Democratic Review* talked about "the fulfilment of our manifest [obvious] destiny" to settle the whole continent from coast to coast. The magazine's editor was John O'Sullivan, and many historians give him credit for coining the well-known term "Manifest Destiny." But evidence shows that the article was written by O'Sullivan's associate, Jane Storm.

In the summer of 1845, General Zachary Taylor and boatloads of U.S.

troops began arriving in the Texas port of Corpus Christi, on the Gulf of Mexico. By the end of the year, about 4,000 men—half of the entire U.S. Army—were camped along the sandy hills by the Nueces River. They drilled for weeks, on the alert, waiting for an enemy attack.

The commander of the Mexican Army of the North, General Mariano Arista, massed his troops at Matamoros, a Gulf port just south of the Rio Grande. He decided to wait for Taylor's troops to move farther into disputed territory, mainly because the Mexican soldiers had few supplies. General Arista complained to his superiors: "[C]onsider that our country and our military honor are going to hell. . . . Consider my situation in the midst of this, asking shops to lend us our daily meals, the officers having nothing to eat."

According to a U.S. informer, supplies headed for General Arista's men were sent secretly to General Mariano Paredes y Arrillaga, who used them for his own troops. Paredes then marched his troops into Mexico City, where John Slidell— President Polk's "peace ambassador"—was trying to meet with President Herrera. Slidell's mission was to pressure Mexico into selling California and New Mexico to the United States. Slidell offered to pay the $2 million in damages claimed earlier by U.S. citizens and a proposed $30 million payment for California and New Mexico. Although President Herrera tried to convince other Mexican officials not to go to war over Texas, he refused to meet with Slidell to discuss the sale of California and New Mexico.

General Paredes forced Herrera to resign, and he took over the presidency. He not only refused Slidell's offers, but he continued to claim that Texas was part of Mexico. Nevertheless, on December 29, 1845, Texas was formally annexed to the United States as the twenty-eighth state.

On January 12, 1846, President Polk learned that Slidell's mission had failed. Polk ordered General Taylor to move his troops toward the Rio Grande, about 150 miles away. On March 8, almost 3,000 soldiers began their march through the disputed territory. Hundreds of soldiers stayed behind. The long, cold winter and poor sanitary conditions in the makeshift army camps had caused many to fall ill with dysentery (a disease that causes severe diarrhea), measles, and other diseases.

Taylor's troops passed the settlement of Point Isabel, burned down by fleeing Mexicans. The troops marched from water hole to water hole in the dry prairie land. They passed a huge herd of wild horses. They passed a party of Mexican soldiers, who merely watched them march by.

Explorer and army captain John Frémont hoped to open up western lands to U.S. expansion and settlement.

Just as Taylor's march began, Captain John Frémont, an explorer and mapmaker with the U.S. Army, led a small group of men from California toward the Oregon border. Known as the Pathfinder, Frémont had already made two expeditions to Oregon Territory, the land along the Pacific Ocean that was north of what Spain had claimed and south of what Russia had claimed. His father-in-law was Senator Thomas Hart Benton, who supported western expansion and wanted to bring U.S. settlers into this region, which Britain also wanted to control.

As part of his third expedition, Frémont arrived in the Sacramento Valley of California in December 1845. He came to Sutter's Fort—a trading post built in 1839 by a Swiss-German immigrant named John Sutter—and informed

General José María Castro, a Mexican military leader in California, of his expedition plans. Castro told Frémont to stay in north-central California within the Sacramento Valley and away from the coast. But in March 1846, Frémont and his men moved south and west to within 25 miles of Monterey, near the coast, and raised the U.S. flag over their camp. Just hours before Castro prepared to attack the camp, Frémont and his men slipped away to the Oregon border.

Meanwhile, Marine Corps lieutenant Archibald Gillespie had left New York City in November 1845 with special orders for Frémont. Gillespie traveled in disguise across Mexico, then sailed to Monterey, California—via Hawaii—to avoid capture by the British navy. Gillespie reached Frémont in southern Oregon in early May. The two adventurers took an instant liking to each other. According to Frémont, Gillespie passed on instructions from the secretary of the navy about gaining California for the United States.

EYEWITNESS QUOTE:
MEN OF PEACE

"They [President Polk and his administration] were men of peace, with objects to be accomplished by means of war."

—Senator Thomas Hart Benton

THE BATTLES BEGIN

On March 28, 1846, General Taylor's troops reached the Rio Grande and raised the U.S. flag on the north side of the river. One of Taylor's officers crossed to the Mexican town of Matamoros on the other side and informed General Pedro de Ampúdia why U.S. troops were there. The general responded by ordering the U.S. Army to remove the flag from Mexican soil. Both sides prepared for battle. Taylor's men built a wooden and earth fort called Fort Texas (later called Fort Brown).

The opposing armies faced each other across the Rio Grande, their artillery within striking distance. Mexican soldiers started crossing the river above and below Fort Texas. The commander at Matamoros, Mariano Arista, ordered General Anatasio Torrejón to lead troops across the Rio Grande. Hearing troop movements, General Taylor ordered Captain Seth Thornton and about 80 dragoons to investigate.

Thornton's men were attacked. Historians differ on the number of U.S. dragoons killed, wounded, and taken prisoner. But they agree that on the next day, April 26, General Torrejón sent a captured dragoon to Taylor to inform him of the skirmish. Taylor then sent a messenger to President Polk with the message that "hostilities may now be considered as commenced."

The first real battle between U.S. and Mexican forces took place about two weeks later. General Taylor mistakenly believed that Mexico's army was attacking his supply base at Point Isabel. He left Major Jacob Brown and about 500 men at Fort Texas and headed with about 2,300 troops to check his supply lines. He got to

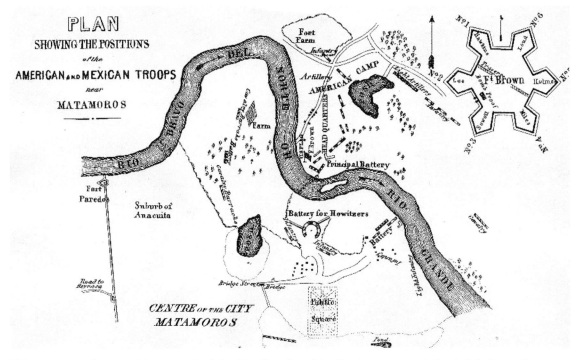

U.S. troops took up positions north of the Rio Grande, while Mexican troops defended their territory to the south near the city of Matamoros. Mexicans called the river Rio Bravo del Norte.

Before war was officially declared, Mexican and U.S. troops fought each other at the Battle of Palo Alto. General Taylor's forces with their more advanced weapons defeated the Mexicans.

Point Isabel the next day without incident and started back with a baggage train of 250 wagons loaded with supplies.

Traveling back toward the fort on May 8, U.S. troops met General Arista's soldiers at a watering hole called Palo Alto. In a battle formation stretching more than a mile along the road stood 6,000 Mexican soldiers—infantry on the left, artillerymen in the middle, cavalry on the right. Outnumbered almost three-to-one, Taylor's troops depended heavily on their artillery, which could shoot three or four rounds per minute. Mexican artillery was older and slower. It could shoot only one or two rounds per minute, and the rounds sometimes fell short of their mark. Under the training of artillery expert Samuel Ringgold, Taylor's artillery squadrons had also developed a way to move light artillery rapidly in any direction and fire with amazing speed. They earned the nickname flying artillery.

Although the Mexican cavalrymen were exceptional fighters, the flying artillery prevented enemy troops from surrounding Taylor's forces and the baggage wagons. Cannonballs from both sides ignited the prairie grasses, and the men fought on through the heat and smoke. By nightfall Arista's troops had taken heavy losses. They retreated, and the U.S. troops were too exhausted to pursue them.

The next day, both armies met again at Resaca de la Palma. General Arista had chosen an excellent position from which to fight. Taylor's men had rested briefly, and they had some food, but the Mexican soldiers had not eaten for at least 30 hours.

Again the fighting was fierce, this time with hand-to-hand combat in dense

EYEWITNESS QUOTE: SAVING MEXICO

"Will the nation allow an enormous piece of its territory to be cut away? Oh! Mexico will be able to save itself only with the strength of its steel and with an invincible determination."

—Antonio López de Santa Anna

Work, Work, Work

James Polk *(right)* was a serious-minded president. He rarely entertained at the White House, and he worked most of his waking hours. For diversion and exercise, he took walks twice a day—once right after sunrise and once about sunset.

chaparral (a dense thicket of small trees and shrubs). As officers lost contact with their men, groups of Mexican soldiers began to retreat. The loss of life for the U.S. Army was greater than at Palo Alto, but Taylor was satisfied. He wrote: "Eight pieces of artillery . . . a great number of prisoners . . . and a large amount of baggage and public property have fallen into our hands."

POLK PUSHES FOR WAR

President Polk knew nothing about Taylor's battles when he called his cabinet (group of advisors) together on May 9. Taylor's messenger was still on his way. John Slidell had reported to him the day before on his failure to buy California and New Mexico. Polk advised his cabinet of Slidell's mission. He announced that he wanted to declare war on Mexico and settle the matter quickly. Secretary of the Navy George Bancroft wanted Polk to wait until Mexico's army attacked, but the rest of the cabinet supported Polk's decision.

After the cabinet meeting ended, Polk received the message General Taylor had sent two weeks earlier, describing how hostilities had started on April 25 against Thornton's scouting party. Rewriting the war message he would send Congress on May 11, Polk felt he had the grounds to say this:

> After repeated menaces, Mexico has passed the boundary of the United States, and shed American blood upon American soil. . . . As war exists, notwithstanding all our efforts to avoid it . . . we are called upon by every consideration of duty and patriotism, to vindicate the honor, the rights, and the interest of our country.

Mexico's Navy

When war broke out, the United States had more than 30 ships in its navy. Mexico had two naval ships in the Gulf: the *Montezuma* and the *Guadalupe*. Mexico gave the ships to the British company that built them so that they would not be captured by U.S. forces.

In other words, the United States was ready to officially declare war on Mexico. Although the House of Representatives quickly voted 174 to 14 to approve the president's recommendations, the Senate was less sure. Some senators doubted whether a president had authority to order troops into disputed territory. Others questioned whether the war was constitutional. Negotiations with Britain over Oregon were not yet complete, and already the president wanted to engage in a war for more territory. Polk had campaigned on the slogan "54–40 or fight," meaning that all the territory south of the latitude of 54 degrees, 40 minutes should belong to the United States. However, as president, Polk supported a treaty with Britain that gave the United States territory only as far north as 49 degrees north latitude.

FAST FACT

POLK'S COMPROMISE

The southern tip of Alaska is about 54 degrees, 40 minutes north latitude. Had Polk stuck to his campaign slogan, the United States would have fought over large parts of southern Canada. The compromise of 49 degrees north latitude is the northern border of Washington, Idaho, Montana, and North Dakota.

In the end, only two senators voted against the war. A third senator, John Calhoun, argued that western expansion and war could destroy the United States by pitting abolitionists (people opposed to slavery) against slave owners, and he withheld his vote. On May 13, 1846, Congress formally declared war against Mexico, set aside $10 million for the war, and called for 50,000 volunteers to join U.S. armed forces.

On the same day, President Polk told Secretary of War William Marcy to send Colonel Stephen Kearny and the Army of the West to occupy Santa Fe, New Mexico (a part of Mexico then). Kearny was stationed at Fort Leavenworth, Kansas Territory—the most western U.S. outpost in 1846. After securing (making safe) Santa Fe, Kearny was to cross the mountains to California, if the weather allowed it.

Less than a week later, the U.S. Army took its first steps into Mexico. General Taylor's army crossed the Rio Grande and occupied the Mexican town of Matamoros—without opposition.

SOLDIERS AND UNIFORMS

U.S. SOLDIERS

The United States did not have a large full-time army when war broke out in 1846. Many of the officers had graduated from the military academy at West Point in New York, and the regular (full-time) soldiers had received some military training. To bring the army up to battle strength, it had to rely on volunteers. About half of the newly enlisted volunteers were recent immigrants, often poor, sometimes unable to read. The regulars were angered by the new troops' lack of training and discipline.

The dress uniform of the regulars in the army was trousers and a short jacket in light blue. Officers had a stripe on their trousers and a darker blue jacket with a red sash. Decorative braids, shoulder boards (broad, stiffened pieces of cloth with a mark of military rank worn on the shoulders of a uniform), and buttons told one corps or rank from another. Some had white belts across their chests. The uniforms were snug, heavy wool, completely unsuitable for Mexico's warm climate. The regular military cap was not practical in Mexico's hot sun, and many officers, including General Zachary Taylor, wore wide-brimmed straw hats instead. Most soldiers carried a rifle or handgun.

U.S. soldiers received a cotton backpack in which to carry a ration of food and a canteen for water, as well as a white belt to hold a bayonet and a cartridge box. The backpack was waterproof. A rolled up coat, which could double as a blanket, was strapped to the top of the backpack.

During the Mexican-American War, dragoons were soldiers who fought on horseback. Dragoons also wore sky-blue trousers. Their jackets were of a heavier material in dark blue, with a double row of gold buttons and shoulder boards with yellow fringe. Dragoons had waist and shoulder belts to carry their swords. In addition to a firearm (gun), dragoons also carried sabers.

A U.S. officer on horseback addresses a group of enlisted infantrymen (foot soldiers).

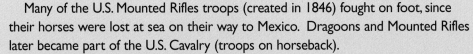

Many of the U.S. Mounted Rifles troops (created in 1846) fought on foot, since their horses were lost at sea on their way to Mexico. Dragoons and Mounted Rifles later became part of the U.S. Cavalry (troops on horseback).

At first, army volunteers had to supply their own clothing, so their dress varied widely. Toward the end of the war, uniforms were available to the volunteers, but few wanted to wear the regular uniform because it was too heavy and hot.

MEXICAN SOLDIERS

Mexico's army was about three times larger than the U.S. Army in 1846. But most of the Mexican soldiers were untrained peasants, Native Americans, or criminals forced into military duty. Many had never fired a gun, since Mexican law forbade the lower classes and Native Americans from owning guns. The average soldier had to provide food and supplies for himself.

Regulations for Mexican uniforms changed several times, and uniforms were in short supply for the regular soldiers. The standard uniform for infantry was a dark blue tailcoat with white canvas pants and a tall stovepipe-shaped hat. Mexican officers often wore French-style uniforms, with a lot of brass and braid. Some cavalry units wore brass helmets with plumes (large, showy feathers).

Many of the officers were educated and well read, but few were trained in military tactics. Officers did not socialize with the regular troops, whom General Antonio López de Santa Anna called "mere chickens."

This illustration shows the variety of uniforms worn by Mexican troops and commanding officers.

3 ROUGH AND READY

Unseasonable rains brought flooding to Matamoros in May and June of 1846. Volunteers for Taylor's army also flooded the town. Some came for the money offered to those who signed up for one year's service. Others came out of a sense of adventure or patriotic duty. By June 12,000 soldiers were sleeping in the open air, swatting the mosquitoes, and practicing for war.

Since Mexican troops deserted Matamoros and no combat took place, some soldiers turned to drinking and gambling. Many in the regular army complained of undisciplined behavior among the newly enlisted men. But Zachary Taylor himself was a relaxed and easygoing

commander. His troops nicknamed him Old Rough and Ready.

While Taylor's troops practiced in Matamoros, Mexican soldiers fought their countrymen in several revolts against the government of Mariano Paredes. Paredes was backed by wealthy aristocrats, who wanted Mexico to return to rule by a king, a monarchy similar to the one established by Augustín de Iturbide when Mexico first gained independence. Even though Paredes probably wanted to avoid a war with the United States, his political supporters thought a war might help their cause. Many antimonarchists (those against a king as leader) reacted violently to the idea of a return to rule by a king. In the middle of this chaos, Native Americans, oppressed by Mexican rule, raided towns in northwestern Mexico. Paredes had to use his troops not only to put down the rebellions but also to conquer the Indians.

In California, revolts against the government in Mexico City had broken out several times since Mexico gained independence. The unrest was often sparked by landowners of Mexican descent (Californios), who preferred to govern themselves and protect their local interests. Most Californios lived near the coast and earned a living by selling hides and tallow (animal fat used for making candles and soap) from their cattle. Californios paid tariffs (taxes) to Mexico City but received little in return in the way of government services or military support. Although many Californios wanted inde-

pendence from Mexico, few wanted the United States to be involved.

By June 1846, rebellion was in the air again in California. This time the unrest came from non-Hispanic (non-Spanish-speaking) immigrants to California who, under Mexican law, were not allowed to own land along the coast. Many of these foreigners had settled in the Sacramento Valley around Sutter's Fort.

THE BEAR FLAG REPUBLIC

After General Castro's encounter with John Frémont's forces in March 1846, rumors spread that Castro had begun to threaten California settlers from the United States, burning their crops and driving off their cattle. Although the rumors were exaggerated, if not entirely false, some U.S. settlers took them seriously. One group from Sutter's Fort attacked a group of Californios and took 150 horses. Another group captured weapons and more horses and took 18 Californios as prisoners.

On June 14, a group of armed men—according to one of them, "about as rough looking a set of men as one could well

Well-known early American artist James Walker painted this portrait of a Californio.

imagine"—gathered in Sonoma and went to the home of Mariano Vallejo, who was the commander of northern California. The men did not know that General Vallejo was secretly working with Thomas Larkin, the U.S. consul (representative) in Monterey, to annex California to the United States. Wishing to avoid further hostility, General Vallejo invited the men in and gave them the keys to his storerooms. But the men had other ideas. They got drunk on Vallejo's brandy and wine, unfolded a strip of linen with a star and a grizzly bear drawn on it, declared California an independent republic, and took Vallejo to Sutter's Fort.

Frémont and his men returned from Oregon just as the Bear Flag Republic was declared. Frémont insisted that Sutter keep Vallejo and three others as prisoners of war. He resigned from the U.S. Army, took charge of the rebellion, and announced that the Bear Flaggers would capture all of California. Appalled by the Bear Flaggers' violent behavior, Larkin observed: "The Bear goes beyond all animals in these parts."

Communications from Mexico City were slow to reach California. Frémont did not know that the United States and Mexico were already at war. In the middle of Frémont's rebellion, Larkin continued to work hard for a bloodless conquest of California. On July 2, the U.S. Pacific Squadron (a fleet of seven battleships) landed in Monterey, California's richest port. Commodore John Sloat, who commanded the squadron, moved in quietly with 250 sailors and marines.

The United States was not the only country interested in claiming California. Great Britain had several military ships off the coast as well. Larkin and Sloat negotiated with British officials interested in taking Monterey in the name of the British king. Sloat and Larkin also assured Californios that an orderly takeover by the U.S. Navy was better than actions by the Bear Flaggers.

On July 7, 1846, the U.S. flag flew over Monterey. U.S. naval captain William

John Frémont and his men raised the Bear Flag (above) in Sonoma, California, in 1846 and claimed California as an independent republic.

A U.S. ship anchored off the coast of Yerba Buena (San Francisco) as part of the effort to claim California for the United States.

Mervine and his men sailed to Yerba Buena (San Francisco) and occupied that town. The United States claimed all of California north of Santa Barbara, including the Bear Flag Republic headquartered at Sutter's Fort. On July 19, Frémont and about 150 Bear Flaggers rode into Monterey and enlisted in the U.S. armed forces as the California Battalion.

Commodore Sloat, who was old and ill, retired in mid-July. He turned his command over to an ambitious young officer named Robert Stockton. Stockton sent the California Battalion by ship to take San Diego and cut off Los Angeles from the south. Stockton and a larger naval force approached Los Angeles from the north, claiming the cities of Santa Barbara and San Pedro along the way.

Los Angeles was only a few miles inland from San Pedro. Californio commander José María Castro had come to Los Angeles for reinforcements after hostilities broke out in northern California. He agreed with Pío Pico, who was the governor of the region, that opposition was useless for the moment. They left Los Angeles.

Stockton and Frémont combined their forces and marched into the town while their military band played the American song, "Hail Columbia."

A few days after occupying Los Angeles, Stockton finally received the formal notice that the United States and Mexico were at war. He declared himself interim (temporary) governor, wrote laws, and set local elections for September. Stockton wrote a letter to President Polk, informing him that "[m]y word is at present the law of the land."

Stockton gave the letter to Kit Carson, a scout with the California Battalion, and Carson started back across the country. On his way east, Carson met Stephen Kearny and his men traveling west. Kearny's Army of the West—about 1,600 men, including 300 dragoons—had set out from Fort Leavenworth, Kansas Territory, in June. With them went light artillery and enough supplies to fill 1,556 wagons.

SANTA FE TRAIL

The Santa Fe Trail was an overland route from western Missouri to Santa Fe, New Mexico. Traders and settlers first used the trail in the 1820s. One branch of the trail followed the Arkansas River to Bent's Fort. The other branch cut through the Cimarron Desert to Fort Union.

Kearny's men rested up at Bent's Fort, a trading post near the border of New Mexico. After war was declared, merchants had gathered there, fearful of using the Santa Fe Trail. Kearny's troops seemed the perfect escort. So when Kearny's men marched into New Mexico Territory on August 2, about 500 wagons filled with civilians and their merchandise went with them.

On August 8, New Mexico governor Manuel Armijo called for armed resistance. More than 3,000 men gathered in Apache Canyon a few miles east of Santa Fe and awaited Kearny's troops. Then Armijo apparently changed his mind and sent the volunteers home. U.S. troops began their occupation of Santa Fe on August 18.

When Carson met up with Brigadier General Kearny (he had been promoted in late June) and gave him Stockton's letter, Kearny passed it on to another soldier to deliver. Then, leaving some troops to keep Santa Fe secure, Kearney and the rest of the troops followed Carson back to California.

TROUBLE

Meanwhile, General Taylor began to move his forces from Matamoros north and westward along the Rio Grande. Some men traveled by steamers, while others rode horses or walked. The army took the town of Reynosa, then continued along the river to Camargo, about 100 miles inland from Matamoros. Taylor stayed at Camargo for six weeks, strengthening his army and preparing to attack Monterrey (not to be confused with Monterey, California).

Food and supplies ran short at Camargo. The temperature hit 112 degrees Fahrenheit. A flood of the Rio Grande contaminated the water. About 1,500 U.S. soldiers died from dysentery and other diseases at Camargo—about as many as the total number of U.S. soldiers who would die in battle during the war.

The Kearny Code

In 1846 U.S. military leader Stephen Kearny *(right)* stood on a roof in Santa Fe and proclaimed:

"People of New Mexico: I have come amongst you . . . to take possession of your country, and extend over it the laws of the United States. . . . Henceforth I absolve you of all allegiance to the Mexican government." Kearny established a set of laws called the Kearny Code. Since there was no treaty with Mexico concerning California, Kearny's actions were illegal.

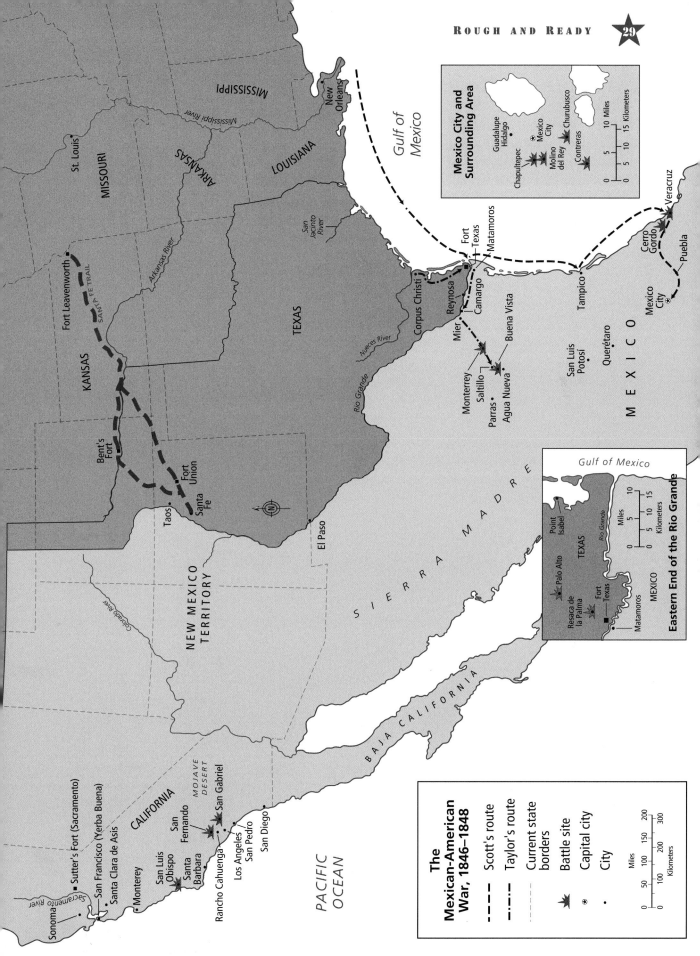

Mexico City and Surrounding Area

Guadalupe
Hidalgo

⊛ Mexico
City

Churubusco

Chapultepec

Molino
del Rey

Contreras

10 Miles

15 Kilometers

5

10

0   5

MISSISSIPPI

New
Orleans

*Gulf of
Mexico*

Veracruz

St. Louis

MISSOURI

ARKANSAS

LOUISIANA

Mississippi River

*San
Jacinto
River*

Fort
Texas

Matamoros

Cerro
Gordo

Puebla

Arkansas River

Corpus Christi

Reynosa

Camargo

Tampico

Mexico
City ⊛

TEXAS

Fort Leavenworth

SANTA FE TRAIL

Nueces River

Mier

Buena Vista

San Luis
Potosí

Querétaro

KANSAS

Rio Grande

Monterrey
Saltillo
Parras •

Agua Nueva

M E X I C O

Bent's
Fort

Fort
Union

Taos •

Santa
Fe

N

El Paso

NEW MEXICO
TERRITORY

S I E R R A   M A D R E

Colorado River

Eastern End of the Rio Grande

Gulf of Mexico

Point
Isabel

Palo Alto

TEXAS

Rio Grande

Resaca de
la Palma

Fort
Texas

Matamoros •

MEXICO

10

5   15

0   5   10   15 Kilometers

Miles

B A J A   C A L I F O R N I A

Sutter's Fort (Sacramento)

San Francisco (Yerba Buena)

Santa Clara de Asis

Monterey

San Luis
Obispo

Santa
Barbara

San
Fernando

San Gabriel

Rancho Cahuenga

Los Angeles
San Pedro

San Diego

CALIFORNIA

*MOJAVE
DESERT*

Sacramento River

Sonoma

*PACIFIC
OCEAN*

**The
Mexican-American
War, 1846–1848**

- - - Scott's route

- · - Taylor's route

———— Current state
borders

✦ Battle site

⊛ Capital city

• City

0   50   100 150 200

Miles

0   100 200 300

Kilometers

Mormon Battalion

Mormons are members of a Christian sect (branch) called the Church of Jesus Christ of Latter-day Saints. They believe that a modern-day prophet, Joseph Smith, received word from God and translated it in the *Book of Mormon* in the early 1800s. Mormon communities sprang up in Ohio and Missouri. Trouble in Ohio led Smith to move to Missouri and to join the Mormons there. Anti-Mormons attacked these settlementes and drove the Mormons from their homes. The Mormons reestablished themselves in Nauvoo, Illinois, in 1838. In 1844 an anti-Mormon mob shot and killed Joseph Smith and attacked other Mormons in Nauvoo.

When President Polk authorized Mormons to enlist in the war with Mexico, the new Mormon leader, Brigham Young *(right),* urged his followers in Nauvoo to sign up and join the march to California. Young saw enlistment as a chance to prove Mormon loyalty to the United States and to move his followers westward at government expense. During July 1846, about 500 men of the Mormon battalion left the military training camp in Iowa. They marched to Fort Leavenworth, Kansas, then to Santa Fe, New Mexico, and across the desert to San Diego, California. Harsh conditions killed several men, but the battalion never engaged in battle. After their discharge in California, most made their way to the Great Salt Lake in Utah, where they joined others in the community who had been forced to leave Nauvoo.

In August, as Taylor moved his remaining men toward Monterrey, Presidents Polk and Paredes each faced political battles over the war. For Polk the issue centered on money. Congressman David Wilmot added an amendment to the bill authorizing an additional $2 million for the war with Mexico. Known as the Wilmot Proviso, the amendment said that slavery would not be alowed in any territory gained from Mexico.

The Wilmot Proviso brought to a boil the conflicts between antislavery and proslavery groups and between those who favored the war and those who opposed it. The House of Representatives passed the bill as Wilmot amended it. But northerners and southerners in the Senate had a tie vote and still hadn't worked out a final decision when Congress ended its work for the season. The Wilmot Proviso would again be introduced at the next session of Congress, but it never became law.

In Mexico, President Paredes had more than an unruly Congress on his hands in August 1846. Valentin Gómez Farías, a political rival who wanted a more democratic government, and José Mariano Salas, a general who opposed Paredes, engineered a successful revolt. Salas became the interim president, and Gómez Farías headed a government council. The new government called for elections in December and other reforms. Many Mexicans were optimistic that the overthrow of Paredes and the change in leadership would bring stability and democracy to Mexico.

Exiled in Cuba, Santa Anna saw his chance to regain power. He allied himself with Salas and Gómez Farías and acted as if he were a believer in democracy. Santa Anna also let President Polk know that a Santa Anna government would consider a treaty giving Texas, California, and New Mexico to the United States in exchange for $30 million, if Polk allowed Santa Anna safe passage to Mexico. President Polk agreed.

On August 16, Santa Anna and his wife sailed through the U.S. blockade of Veracruz to what a British observer called a "cool reception, for not one *viva* [Spanish for Long Live!] was heard." Santa Anna worked his way into becoming part of the new government.

On September 14, Santa Anna and Gómez Farías entered Mexico City together. With Salas as interim president, Santa Anna assumed command of Mexico's army. He stayed in the capital for two weeks, raising money for his troops. Before he was finished raising money, the battle for Monterrey was over.

General Antonio López de Santa Anna regained control of Mexico's army after negotiating safe passage through the U.S. blockade at Veracruz.

WEAPONS OF THE MEXICAN-AMERICAN WAR

Weapons and their use were changing at about the time of the Mexican-American War. In general, U.S. troops had more advanced models and techniques than Mexico's army, which had outdated weapons from the 1821 war with Spain or had surplus weapons from other countries.

Most common among the Mexican infantry were the Brown Bess flintlock musket and the Baker flintlock rifle. To load these guns, a soldier first tore open a paper cartridge containing a ball and gunpowder. He sprinkled some of the powder on the flintlock pan at the back of the gun and the rest down its muzzle. The he shoved the ball and paper wrapping into the muzzle with a ramrod. The trigger released a hammer, which struck a flint, causing a spark that ignited the powder. The powder exploded and fired the ball.

The .75 caliber (diameter of the barrel) Brown Bess was smoothbore (smooth interior of the barrel), while the .625 caliber Baker rifle had a rifled bore—spiraled grooves cut into the bore, which sent the ball farther and with greater accuracy.

The most common rifle used by the U.S. infantry was the Model 1841 rifle, .54 caliber with a 33-inch-long barrel. It was more powerful than the Baker rifle. The Baker was the most accurate rifle used by either army. It was called the Mississippi rifle because it was often carried by volunteers from Mississippi.

Both U.S. and Mexican soldiers used bayonets when fighting at close range. They attached bayonets to the front of their rifles. A bayonet weighed about two pounds and made rifles less accurate. Sometimes the blast out of a rifle's muzzle also dislodged or damaged the bayonet.

Much of the fighting during the Mexican-American War took place at close range. Soldiers fought each other with rifles, bayonets, and sabers.

U.S. mounted troops *(above)* often carried the Model 1833 saber (sword), known as the Old Wrist Breaker because of the weight of its two-pound blade. They also might carry the Model 1819 or 1836 pistol, a muzzle-loading (single shot) .54 caliber gun. Some had Colt revolvers, usually the .44 caliber Walker model. Mexican mounted troops often carried a lance and a saber that was lighter than the U.S. saber.

In 1840 U.S. Secretary of War Joel Poinsett sent officers to Europe to study advances in artillery and to bring back more modern cannons. At the start of the Mexican-American War, the United States used the most advanced techniques. Cannons were made from bronze, which was more reliable and lighter than cannons made from iron. Mexico had older iron artillery and less expertise in using modern weaponry.

Common U.S. artillery was the Model 1840 family of weapons, ranging in weight from 880 pounds to up to 5,600 pounds. These included:

• 6-pounder (weight of the cannonball) cannons
• 12-pounder howitzers (slightly smaller than a cannon)
• 8- and 10-inch mortars (artillery that can lob balls over high obstacles)

The Mexican mounted troops were often well trained and effective. But Mexico's army didn't have any light, mobile artillery such as the U.S. flying artillery. The flying artillery men rode their own horses, while other horses pulled the lighter guns—usually the 6-pounder cannon. The gun crew took only a few minutes to gallop into position, dismount, set, aim, and fire the cannon, then remount and move to another position. Often the flying artillery made the difference between victory and defeat in battles with Mexico's army.

MONTERREY

While Taylor's troops were drilling and dying in Camargo, Mexico's army recovered from its early defeats. General Pedro de Ampúdia replaced General Arista, enlisted 5,000 men, and arrived in Monterrey just ahead of Taylor's force of 6,600.

Ampúdia set up headquarters in the cathedral in the center of Monterrey, a well-fortified walled city of 20,000 nestled in the mountains of the Sierra Madre. He filled the cathedral with ammunition and sent artillery and men to defend areas in and around the city. Mountains formed a natural barrier in the south, with a single narrow road leading to the town of Saltillo. Two hills—Independence and Federation—and a fortress called the Citadel, guarded the northern approach to the city.

General Taylor divided his forces in half. General William Worth's half was supposed to close off the road to Saltillo, then capture the two fortified hills. Taylor's half would create a diversion by launching an attack on the Citadel.

On September 20—the 250th anniversary of Monterrey's founding in 1596—the United States attacked. General Worth overpowered Mexican forces, sealed off the Saltillo

> ### EYEWITNESS QUOTE: TRAINING CAMP
>
> "July 6.—Nothing today of importance, drill four hours a day.
>
> July 7.—A great deal of complaining about rations in bread.
>
> July 8.—Almost everyone complaining about diarrhea.
>
> July 10.—Strong talk with some of deserting."
>
> —Thomas D. Tennery, volunteer soldier, training camp in Illinois, 1846

General Worth's troops marched up the Saltillo road from the west toward Monterrey.

On September 23, 1846, U.S. troops broke through the outer walls of Monterrey and faced fierce gunfire.

road, and captured Federation, the smaller of the two hills. Taylor's troops miscalculated their position and got caught in crossfire between the Citadel and another fort.

In a fierce battle, Taylor's men finally forced Ampúdia's troops toward the center of the city. That night during a rainstorm, Worth's men stormed Independence Hill. Mexican artillery on the hill was aimed too high, allowing U.S. troops to crawl under it and overpower the defenders at the top. Then Worth's men turned the big guns on the city.

General Ampúdia ordered his troops to concentrate their forces in the city, although the Citadel was still in Mexican hands. Taylor's forces broke through the city's walls and encountered heavy fighting. Then U.S. troops pulled back to the edges of the city and continued to bombard the central city throughout the night. Fearing that his ammunition-filled headquarters would explode, Ampúdia asked for a truce.

The U.S. and Mexican troops arranged an eight-week armistice, a temporary stop to the fighting. Ampúdia's army surrendered the Citadel and left the city, taking with them personal arms and a few light weapons. Santa Anna and his troops were partway to Monterrey when they learned of the battle and armistice. Since he was near San Luis Potosí, Santa Anna decided to gather Mexico's army there and prepare an assault against Taylor's men after the armistice was over.

EYEWITNESS QUOTE: BATTLE OF MONTERREY

"The wind of passing balls and bombs continually fanned their faces. . . . A twelve-pound shot literally passed through the closed ranks of the Tennessee regiment, throwing fragments of human beings into the air, and drenching the living with gore."

—Thomas Thorpe, U.S. war correspondent, September 20, 1846

CONTINUING CONFLICT

4

The armistice that Generals Taylor and Ampúdia arranged brought relief from fighting in northeastern Mexico in September and October of 1846. But violence erupted in California. Angered by military rule imposed on them by John Frémont, Robert Stockton, and Archibald Gillespie, about 600 Californios attacked Gillespie and 50 soldiers camped near Los Angeles. Gillespie surrendered to their leader, José María Flóres, and retreated with his men to Monterey, California.

Commodore Stockton, who was in Monterey then, ordered a U.S. naval force under Captain Mervine to attack Los Angeles. But Californios prevented Mervine's men from taking the city. Stockton decided to change his base of operations to San Diego in hopes of retaking Los Angeles from the south.

When President Polk learned of Taylor's armistice at Monterrey, Mexico, he was furious. Polk wanted a quick end to the war, especially since congressional elections were coming in November. Polk ordered Taylor not to extend the armistice and to stay put. Instead, when the armistice was over, Taylor marched his men into Saltillo. This strategically placed town of about 10,000 had been abandoned by enemy troops. General John Wool captured the nearby town of Parras and joined Taylor at Saltillo. Commodore David Conner took over the port of Tampico, also abandoned by Mexican forces.

Saltillo and Tampico fell into U.S. hands so easily because Santa Anna had ordered Mexican troops to abandon their positions around the country and gather at San Luis Potosí. With Taylor's forces at Saltillo and Santa Anna's at San Luis Potosí, the opposing armies were only about a two-week march from each other.

General Taylor proposed that the United States concentrate on holding only the northeastern part of Mexico, rather than risking the 1,000-mile trek into Mexico City. But this tactic did not seem to bring about the surrender and treaty terms that Polk wanted—that Mexico give up about half its territory. Also, true to Polk's prediction, congressional elections brought more antiwar Whig candidates to power and made it even harder for the president to get the votes he wanted to continue the war.

President Polk had decided that the only way to bring a quick and favorable end to the war was for U.S. forces to march on Mexico City. He didn't want to give the opportunity to Taylor. Success on the battlefield would make the popular general even more popular and would make him a likely opponent in the presidential election of 1848. Another possibility was Major General Winfield Scott. Scott was less well known than Taylor and would be less of a threat in the elections. So, shortly after the elections, Polk ordered Scott to take half of Taylor's troops and prepare to lead them for an attack on Mexico City.

> EYEWITNESS QUOTE: MEASLES
>
> "November 22 [1846]. Today we saw the corpse of a boy who had died of measles. They are very fatal at present among the Mexican children, who have caught them from the soldiers."
>
> —Thomas D. Tennery, Illinois Volunteers, Matamoros, Mexico

FAST FACT

WHIGS

Popular in the 1830s and 1840s, the Whig Party was the rival of the Democratic Party. By the 1850s, the issue of slavery divided the Whigs. Many southern Whigs joined with the proslavery Democrats. Northern Whigs started the antislavery Republican Party.

General Winfield Scott (center) reviews his troops.

Napoleon Dana

One of the soldiers Scott took from Taylor's command, Lieutenant Napoleon Dana, wrote to his wife, "We have parted from our brave old chief. . . . As we are going to join General Scott, we will expect to have to pay more attention to the regulations of dress, hair, whiskers, and so forth. . . . I shaved off my beard . . . this afternoon." Dana was later wounded and left for dead for two days before being brought back to camp by a burial party. He recovered.

At about the same time, the Mexican government held the elections that interim president Salas had promised after the overthrow of General Paredes. Despite political pressures from different factions in the government, the alliance between Santa Anna and Gómez Farías managed to survive. Santa Anna was elected president, and Gómez Farías became his vice president. Santa Anna returned to his military command at San Luis Potosí, leaving Gómez Farías in charge of the government.

RECONQUERING CALIFORNIA AND NEW MEXICO

Meanwhile, Kearny's dragoons had dragged themselves and two cannons across hundreds of miles of mountains and deserts from Santa Fe to southern California. In early December, the dragoons finally made it to Warner's Ranch, about 40 miles from San Diego. Kearny thought that all of California was still in American hands. When he found out it wasn't, he sent a message to Stockton in San Diego. Stockton sent Gillespie, and a small force met them. They fought Californios in the mountainous area near San Pasqual, where both Kearny and Gillespie were wounded in a battle. Cannon fire from U.S. forces caused the Californios to retreat.

Kearny's and Stockton's forces assembled at San Diego. Kearny outranked Stockton. But most of the troops had been under Stockton's command and Stockton knew the area, so the two men shared command. At the end of December, the U.S. troops set out for Los Angeles.

New Year's Day 1847 brought U.S. Marines to settlers barricaded inside the Catholic mission compound (church resi-

Commodore Robert Stockton declared himself temporary governor of California in July 1846.

After marching 140 miles from San Diego to Los Angeles, U.S. troops fought angry Californios at the Battle of San Gabriel in January 1847.

dences and other buildings) at Santa Clara de Asis in northern California. Although this part of California was under the control of the United States, hostilities had not completely ended. Some of the settlers had left families there and joined Frémont's California Battalion. Among the women who stayed behind was Olive Mann Isbell. The niece of educator Horace Mann, Isbell had set up a school for the settlers' children trapped at Santa Clara mission. She and the children cleaned a stable and made benches and a table from scrap wood. Isbell wrote lessons on the dirt floor with a stick and drew letters on the children's hands with pieces of charred wood. She was probably California's first American teacher, and the Santa Clara stable became California's first English-speaking school.

Armed with a small cannon, the U.S. Marines spread out near the Santa Clara de Asis mission and waited for an attack by Don Francisco Sanchez and his horsemen.

These Californios sought revenge for a U.S. supply raid on the Sanchez ranch. In the fighting that followed, the marines repelled Sanchez's attack. Only one person died—a marine who was killed when his gun blew up. A truce then ended fighting in northern California.

The fighting for southern California ended a few days later. Although Los Angeles was only about 140 miles from San Diego, it took U.S. forces more than a week to get there. The men made canvas shoes to trek across the deep sand at the edge of the Mojave Desert, and it was slow going. Flóres sent word to Stockton that the Californios wanted a truce that would keep Flóres as governor until a peace treaty was signed. Stockton refused.

With only about 450 poorly armed men, Flóres made his stand on a ridge near the San Gabriel River, about 12 miles from Los Angeles. The 90-minute battle that afternoon ended with defeat and retreat for the Californios.

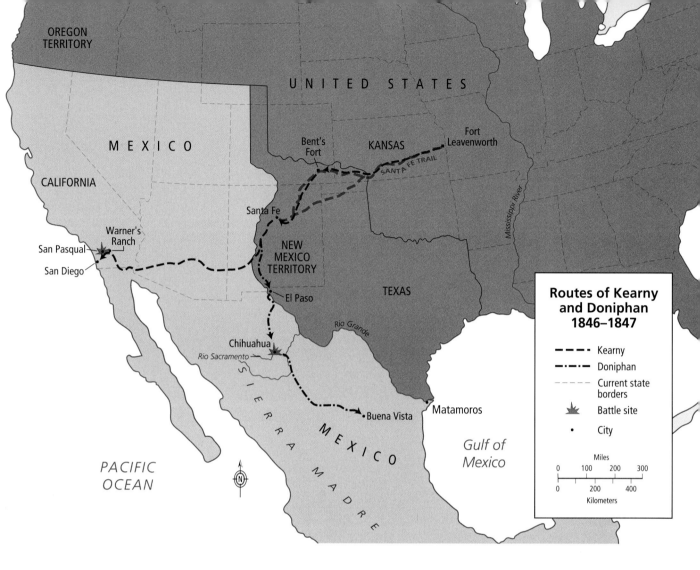

Routes of Kearny
and Doniphan
1846–1847

- – – – Kearny
- – · – · Doniphan
- – – – Current state borders
- ✳ Battle site
- • City

Miles
0   100   200   300

0   200   400
Kilometers

The day after the Battle of San Gabriel, U.S. forces fought on the broad mesa (flat-topped hills) along the San Fernando River and won again. They reached Pío Pico's ranch, but no Californios were there. Pío Pico had decided to flee to Mexico to avoid capture. On January 10, Los Angeles surrendered.

About four days later, Frémont and the California Battalion showed up in Los Angeles. They told Stockton that they had fought at San Luis Obispo, captured Jesús Pico (a cousin of Pío Pico), and used him to persuade Flóres and the last of his men from Los Angeles to surrender. Flóres

transferred his governorship to Andrés Pico (the brother of Pío Pico) and left for Sonora. Frémont and Andrés Pico then drafted a truce at Rancho Cahuenga.

Frémont showed Stockton the Treaty of Cahuenga, signed by Pico for California and by Frémont for the United States. Frémont had no authority to represent the United States, and the treaty's terms were more favorable to the Californios than Stockton wanted. But Stockton accepted the treaty anyway.

Stockton appointed Frémont military governor of California even though Kearny argued that President Polk had ordered him

(Kearny) to conquer California. Tensions mounted among the U.S. military leaders.

William Branford Shubrick, who was in charge of a naval blockade of California, landed in Monterey. In early February, Commodore Shubrick replaced Stockton as the highest-ranking naval officer and lifted the martial law (rule by the military) that U.S. forces had imposed during the capture of California.

Commodore Shubrick shared responsibility for governing California with Stephen Kearny, a brigadier general in the army. Kearny then met with Colonel Richard Mason, who arrived with orders from the president to take over the governorship as soon as hostilities had ended. Angered at losing his authority over California, Frémont challenged Mason to a duel but finally accepted Polk's orders.

For the past few months, unrest had been building in Santa Fe, New Mexico. Kearny had arranged for Charles Bent to become the provisional (temporary) governor of the terri-

Colonel Alexander Doniphan

tory, angering many of the Mexicans and Indians there. The troops stationed at Santa Fe under Colonel Alexander Doniphan were a rowdy bunch, often harassing the local citizens. Colonel Sterling Price and his men arrived and relieved Doniphan and his troops. Doniphan's men then left Santa Fe to make treaties with local Native American groups on behalf of the U.S. government.

On January 19, a mob of Native Americans gathered at the home of Governor Bent in Taos, a trading post about 80 miles north of Santa Fe. Declaring that no U.S. citizen would govern New Mexico, they killed Bent, but left his wife and other houseguests unharmed. The Native

Colt Revolvers

In 1830, when he was 16, Samuel Colt designed his first revolver—a gun that had five chambers for bullets rather than the single muzzled-loaded pistol popular with the U.S. Army. The revolver was manufactured in Paterson, New Jersey, and was called the Colt Paterson. Although the Paterson was difficult to load on horseback and was relatively fragile, some U.S. Army volunteers bought the guns to take to war in Mexico in 1846. Zachary Taylor ordered Captain Samuel Walker, a former Texas Ranger (a state militia formed when Texas was part of Mexico), to work with Colt to make a better model. The Walker Model came out in 1847 and was distributed to five companies of U.S. dragoons. Colt created the designs for thousands of handguns later used during the U.S. Civil War (1861–1865).

An advertisement for the Paterson Colt revolver

Americans were joined by others, and they seemed to be preparing to attack Santa Fe.

Colonel Price waited for reinforcements. Then, on February 2, he attacked the rebels at Taos Pueblo, a 300-year-old Native American town near Taos. After being shelled by artillery for two days, the rebels surrendered. About a dozen leaders were hanged. Resentment over U.S. rule continued in New Mexico, but rebellions ended.

TAYLOR'S LAST BATTLES

The new year brought new troubles for Zachary Taylor. He had a hard time getting supplies to U.S. troops stationed at Saltillo and other outposts in northeast Mexico. To make matters worse, General Scott had taken about half of Taylor's forces—most of Taylor's best men—for the invasion of Mexico City. That left Taylor with only 6,000 men, mainly inexperienced volunteers.

An ad calls for volunteers from New Hampshire (known as the Granite State). Many of the men fighting in the Mexican-American War were volunteer soldiers.

When Santa Anna learned that Taylor had lost half his men, the Mexican general decided the time was right to attack. About 20,000 Mexican soldiers were at San Luis Potosí, more than three times Taylor's force. When Taylor learned that Santa Anna's army was on the move, he decided to face the enemy in a place easier to defend.

Taylor's troops moved south from Saltillo to Agua Nueva. There they rested, drank fresh water, and drilled, practicing marching and maneuvers. U.S. scouts reported Santa Anna's progress from San Luis Potosí.

When Mexican forces were a day away from Agua Nueva, Taylor's men retreated a few miles north to a mountain pass selected by General Wool, near the hacienda (large estate or plantation) of Buena Vista. Santa Anna's forces had traveled 100 miles over harsh terrain in bitter weather before they reached Agua Nueva. Manuel Balbontín, a Mexican officer, later wrote: "It [was] very cold. Windy and snowing. Last night some of the soldiers and women died from exposure. The troops were so hungry and numb that they refused to march."

When the exhausted Mexican troops reached Agua Nueva and Santa Anna saw how recently the U.S. troops had been camped there, he urged his army forward. The soldiers did not have time to refill their canteens or to rest. In the meantime, U.S. troops waited on General Wool's carefully selected battlefield. Mountains and

Translating Taylor

Before the battle of Buena Vista, Santa Anna sent a note to General Zachary Taylor suggesting that Taylor surrender. Taylor ordered a staff officer to "tell Santa Anna to go to hell." Instead, the officer wrote this response to Santa Anna in Spanish: "In reply to your note of this date summoning me to surrender. . . . I beg leave to say that I decline acceding to your request."

hills prevented any military action from one side. Several ravines on the other side made it difficult for Mexico's army to use its strong and deadly cavalry effectively.

By February 22, 1847, the two armies faced each other. Included among the Mexican troops was a group of soldiers flying a green silk banner embroidered with a silver cross and golden harp. This was the Battalia San Patricio (Saint Patrick Battalion), a company of deserters from the U.S. Army. Many of the deserters were Irish Catholic immigrants who had recently come to the United States because of the failure of the potato crop and resulting famine in Ireland. They had faced anti-Catholic prejudice in the U.S. Army and were encouraged by Mexican propaganda to join the ranks of fellow Catholics defending Mexico against the Protestant invaders from the north.

Santa Anna gave Taylor a chance to surrender, but the U.S. general refused. Two

days of fierce fighting followed, with Mexico's army often on the offensive. By the end of the second day, U.S. artillery had barely managed to hold off a major attack. Retreat was difficult in the mountainous terrain, and there was little hope of reinforcements.

Taylor's troops spent an anxious night, with the fires of the Mexican camp in full view. But by dawn on February 24, Mexico's army was gone. The fires had been built to fool U.S. troops as Santa Anna's forces retreated to Agua Nueva during the night. According to accounts, the U.S. troops shouted with joy, and Generals Wool and Taylor embraced each other with tears in their eyes.

Mexico's army had suffered about 2,100 casualties, which meant that they still had many more men than the U.S. forces had. Santa Anna might have reasoned that Taylor would follow him to Agua Nueva, where Mexican forces would be effective in open ground. But Taylor did not take the bait.

After resting a day at Agua Nueva, Santa Anna marched his troops west, through the desert, to La Encarnación. Many wounded soldiers died along the way. What was left of Mexico's army then returned to San Luis Potosí.

Both sides claimed victory at the battle of Buena Vista. Santa Anna was later criticized for retreating at the mountain pass. After resting his troops at Agua Nueva, Taylor and his men retreated to Monterrey and stayed there. The two generals never fought each other again.

EYEWITNESS QUOTE: SURGEON'S WORK

"Under the cliffs at the pass the Surgeon and his assistants were busy preparing amputating tables."

—U.S. soldier, right before the battle of Buena Vista, February 22, 1847

THE HOME FRONT

U.S. citizens were deeply divided about waging war with Mexico. Many people of the Lone Star Republic—formerly the Mexican state of Texas—were eager to join the United States and to gain additional territory from Mexico. In general, people in the southern states favored the war. Jefferson Davis, a congressman from Mississippi, received these words in a letter from one of his voters: "We are in great excitement, drums beating, fifes playing, flags flying, meetings holding, and 'To Arms To Arms,' in large Capitals stuck up at every corner of the streets, and at every fork in the roads."

GOING TO AND RETURNING FROM MEXICO.

This antiwar cartoon shows a healthy, uniformed soldier ready to go to Mexico and wounded soldiers hobbling back home.

Many in the northern states opposed the war, in part because they saw it as a means to extend slavery. Former president John Quincy Adams described the war as a way for the South to get "bigger pens to cram with slaves." *New York Tribune* editor Horace Greeley called the war "atrocious."

By December 1846, about 300,000 men had volunteered to join the armed forces as their patriotic duty, as a way to have an adventure, or as a means to feed their families. As one-year volunteers returned home maimed or ill, the war became less and less popular. President Polk wrote in his diary that he was "perfectly disgusted with the want [lack] of patriotism" in Congress. Congressmen reflected the attitude of their voters, many of whom felt that the United States should not be in a war with Mexico.

5 CONQUERING PEACE

Having signed treaties with several Native American groups in New Mexico, Colonel Doniphan sat in El Paso, Texas, and waited to hear from General Wool. The plan was for the men and their troops to meet near Chihuahua, in north-central Mexico, and invade the city. Then plans changed.

Wool's forces were needed at Saltillo instead. Doniphan could rest up in El Paso or make the 300-mile trek to Chihuahua, over mountains and through deserts, and take his chances without reinforcements. Doniphan called his men together and put it to a vote. He had volunteered for service, like the rest of his regiment, the 1st Missouri Mounted Infantry. They elected

him their leader and had a say in almost everything. This time, they chose to go to Chihuahua.

In early February 1847, a few other soldiers arrived with six pieces of artillery. About 1,000 U.S. soldiers left El Paso along with a train of 315 wagons filled with civilians and their goods all heading to Chihuahua.

Mexican general García Condé got to Chihuahua first. With him were more than 2,000 soldiers. On February 28, Condé set up artillery on a plateau just north of the Sacramento River, facing the road Doniphan's troops and wagon train would be taking. There was a dry riverbed below the plateau and mountains on either side

45

of the road. Condé waited for Doniphan to march down the road, but that wasn't Doniphan's plan.

Doniphan's scouts found a rough trail up the side of the plateau, out of range of Mexican artillery. It took several grueling hours to push-pull wagons and artillery up the steep sides. By the time Condé's men realized what had happened, Doniphan's force had made it to the top, behind enemy lines. The Missouri volunteers fired their artillery, then fought fiercely in hand-to-hand combat. The Mexican troops retreated, leaving only one U.S. soldier dead.

Doniphan marched into Chihuahua the next day. Most of the Mexican residents had fled. The Missouri volunteers moved in and made a mess, turning houses into stables and the public drinking fountain into a bathtub. Susan Magoffin, who came with her merchant husband in the wagon train, wrote in her diary that the men "are

not careful at all how much they soil the property of a friend much less an enemy."

THE "WOMAN'S REVOLUTION"

Unlike residents who had abandoned Chihuahua, many of the 15,000 residents of Veracruz stayed in their port city and watched U.S. forces gathering offshore. For months, boatloads of military men and supplies arrived on the Island of Lobos, just behind the American blockade line. Juan Morales, the general in charge of the Veracruz garrison, kept asking for more soldiers, but none came. Santa Anna's troops were busy elsewhere, and the government in Mexico City had problems of its own.

In January Vice President Gómez Farías had tried to raise money for the army by requiring the Catholic Church to sell off some property. This action angered many in the church and their supporters, who threatened to overthrow the government.

U.S. troops gathered troops off the coast of Veracruz in preparation for attack.

On February 25, Gómez Farías ordered five battalions of militia in Mexico City to reinforce Morales's troops at Veracruz. These battalions stayed in Mexico City instead and waged a civil war against the government.

Santa Anna probably organized this revolt as a way to gain more power. The revolt might also have been part of a plan worked out by Santa Anna, other Mexicans, U.S. secret agent Moses Y. Beach, and journalist Jane Storm. Under the plan, General Scott was to demonstrate the superior military strength of the United States by attacking Veracruz. Then there was to be a crisis within the government. Santa Anna, as a national hero who knew how to save face and keep his people's honor, would negotiate peace.

The peace would include three independent republics within Mexico; U.S. annexation of California, New Mexico, and Texas; U.S. rights to use the Tehuantepec Isthmus in southern Mexico; and plenty of foreign aid. About 125 miles wide at its narrowest point, the isthmus (narrow strip of land) seemed a good place to build a canal to connect shipping in the Atlantic and Pacific Oceans. (The Panama Canal later proved to be easier to construct.)

U.S. agent Moses Beach called the scheme the "woman's revolution" because much of it was journalist Jane Storm's idea. In the months before the attack on Veracruz, Scott knew nothing of what Beach, Storm, and officials in Washington and Mexico City had secretly planned to carry out. Scott planned the invasion of Veracruz as the first step on the road to Mexico City.

The Mexican capital stood on the site of the ancient city of Tenochtitlán, home of the sixteenth-century Aztec ruler Montezuma. Scott chose the same route taken by Spanish invader Hernán Cortés when Cortés marched troops into Tenochtitlán in 1519. Like Cortés, the U.S. forces would start at Veracruz and march inland through the marshes, then up into the hills and mountains surrounding the Valley of Mexico, with Mexico City in the middle.

Tenochtitlán was the ancient capital city of the Aztec Empire. The Spaniards destroyed Tenochtitlán in the 1500s and built Mexico City in its place.

Yellow Fever

Yellow fever is a disease caused by a virus transmitted by mosquitoes that have bitten infected humans or monkeys. In mild cases, the patient recovers completely. In severe cases, the disease causes liver failure, massive bleeding, and death. Victims vomit frequently and have blood in their vomit, from which comes the Spanish name *vómito* or "black vomit" in English. They also have high fever and a jaundiced (yellow) skin, from which comes the other English name, yellow fever.

Scott worried that his men would fall victim to vómito—yellow fever. Although it would be decades before a Cuban physician proved that mosquitoes carried the disease, Scott knew that yellow fever occurred most often in the spring and summer months in swamps and coastal areas. He timed his invasion of Mexico City so that his troops would be gone from the coastal plains by April. Scott also asked Surgeon General Thomas Lawson to join him on the invasion.

By March about 12,000 U.S. troops stood ready to attack Veracruz. President Polk once described Scott as "rather scientific and visionary in his views," and the Veracruz invasion proved Polk right. Scott worked closely with Commodore David Conner to combine the best use of army and navy forces. Scott and Conner worked out a set of new signals that both sailors and soldiers could understand. The army and navy developed landing procedures and designed small double-ended surfboats to take soldiers and supplies ashore. The invasion of Veracruz was the largest amphibious (land and sea) operation that U.S. military forces ever conducted until World War II (1939–1945).

Surfboats carried U.S. troops to the beaches in the invasion of Veracruz.

Surfboats

On General Scott's orders, navy lieutenant George M. Totten designed a surfboat, the first specially built U.S. landing craft, for the invasion of Veracruz. The surfboats were built in Philadelphia for the army's Quartermaster Department and cost $795 each—a huge amount then. Scott ordered 141 surfboats, but only 65 arrived in time, packed one inside another in three sizes (from 35 feet 9 inches to 40 feet) for easy shipment. Each double-ended, flat-bottomed boat had an eight-man crew and could carry 40 soldiers or horses and artillery.

On March 1, news came of Santa Anna's "victory" at Buena Vista. Santa Anna was once again a national hero. According to the peace plan arranged by Beach and Storm, Scott's attack on Veracruz was supposed to have happened before Santa Anna's return to Mexico City. But even General Scott could not control the weather.

Late winter storms delayed the Veracruz invasion, and the peace plan began to falter. While Beach waited for Santa Anna to arrive in Mexico City, Storm left for Veracruz to give Scott the details of her plan.

VERACRUZ

The sky cleared over Veracruz on March 9, 1847. Residents lined the walls of their fortified city to watch the first surfboats of U.S. troops head for shore. After they landed, Scott's troops circled the city, cutting off food and water supplies. Over the next week, wagons, horses, oxen, artillery, and military bands went ashore. The bands played rousing tunes as soldiers took up their positions around Veracruz.

Scott thought his troops might be attacked as they landed, but General Morales chose not to. He had less than half the number of soldiers that Scott had and preferred to take a defensive position within the city's strong fortifications.

On March 21, Jane Storm arrived in Veracruz after traveling six long days from Mexico City. She told Scott about the peace plan and how his attack on Veracruz would be immediately followed by peace negotiations. She showed him a list in code of influential Mexicans who supported the plan.

But Scott hardly paid any attention. His orders were to take Mexico City. He refused to linger near the coast while government officials haggled over a treaty. Time was running out if he wanted to avoid yellow fever.

The next day, Scott demanded that Morales surrender Veracruz. When Morales refused, Scott started a barrage of cannon fire from four sites around the city. Mexican troops along the city walls fired back but were no match for Scott's 8-inch howitzers, 10-inch mortars, and 24-pound siege guns. The shelling set fires within the city. But the solid walls surrounding Veracruz held.

Scott asked for six huge naval cannons with 32-pound shells to be brought

EYEWITNESS QUOTE: PEACE TREATY

"If . . . [General] Scott will use no argument but the sword, it will cost many lives, much treasure, and much time to conquer peace."

—Jane Storm, journalist

Montgomery's Mission

A young widow with land in Texas and influential contacts in Washington, D.C., Jane McManus Storm wrote newspaper columns under the name Cora Montgomery. The columns were published in the *Sun,* which in 1846 had the most readers of any newspaper in the world. Storm arranged for *Sun* publisher Moses Y. Beach to receive a letter from Secretary of State James Buchanan stating that the president appointed Beach "confidential agent to the Republic of Mexico."

Storm, Beach, and Beach's daughter Drusilla sailed to Cuba, where they met with Mexicans and received British passports. After weeks of negotiation, they reached Mexico City in January 1847. There they began secret talks with the Mexican priests and government officials to annex parts of Mexico to the United States and end the war. Storm used a series of Montgomery columns titled "Tropical Sketches" to tell U.S. government officials about the mission's progress.

Disguised as a British banker, Moses Beach printed an announcement of a grand ball. The guest list for the ball named in code the people he and Storm thought supported their scheme. Storm was fluent in Spanish and petite, with black hair and a dark complexion. Except for her violet eyes, she blended into the Mexican population. So she was the logical choice to take the list to General Scott in Veracruz and reveal Beach's mission.

These two soldiers, **Captains William Chapman** *(left)* **and Moses Merrill** *(right),* **fought for the U.S. Army during the Battle of Veracruz.**

ashore. Commodore Matthew Perry, who had relieved Commodore Conner, did as ordered. Each cannon weighed three tons, and it took more than 200 men to drag each of them over three miles of beach to within half a mile of the city walls. Scott opened fire, and the walls began to give way.

Morales resigned rather than surrender. On March 26, Brigadier General José Juan Landero called a truce. By then Scott had bombarded the city with about 6,700 shells. Jane Storm watched the shelling from the crowded deck of the British warship HMS *Daring,* which took British civilians on board during the U.S. attack. Storm noted that Spanish and French ships in the harbor did the same for other foreign civilians who were residents of Veracruz.

Meanwhile, Beach waited in Mexico City for news about Storm and a "peace envoy" from the United States. Santa Anna had returned but refused to enter Mexico City until the revolt ended. In an artful game of double dealing, Santa Anna broke with Gómez Farías and overturned the order to sell church property. He had the Mexican Congress abolish the position of vice president, thus ousting (removing by force) Gómez Farías. And he again made himself president.

Instead of calling for negotiations as he had promised, Santa Anna changed his position and pushed for war. The church pledged to contribute $2 million to support the army.

EYEWITNESS QUOTE: VERACRUZ

"It was awful! My heart bled for the inhabitants. The soldiers I did not care so much for, but it was terrible to think of the women and children."

—Captain Robert E. Lee, watching the shelling of Veracruz

On March 25, with no news about Veracruz or a peace envoy, Beach sent a message to Washington that the "woman's revolution" had failed.

Soon afterward, Beach received an invitation from Santa Anna to meet with him. The U.S. consul in Mexico City warned Beach that the meeting was a deadly trap. That night, Beach and his daughter, who had accompanied him to Mexico, abandoned their possessions and took what was to look like a leisurely ride to a nearby hacienda. Instead, they fled on horseback to U.S.-held Tampico about 300 miles away. Posters went up offering a $500 reward for the capture of the "Yankee Spy, named M. Y. Beach, who under the guise of an Englishman has been plotting against the peace of Mexico."

This old print pictures the citizens of the city of Veracruz during the U.S. bombardment in March 1847.

WOMEN IN THE MEXICAN-AMERICAN WAR

Although generally not soldiers, many women followed the U.S. and Mexican troops during the 1846–1848 war. Their motives included patriotism, protection, personal ties, and profits. Wives of enlisted men were allowed to stay with their husbands and enroll in the U.S. Army as laundresses and cooks. The most famous of these was Sarah Borginnis Bowman, a crack shot who became a lieutenant in the army. Women had an informal but vital role in Mexico's army as *soldaderas.* They found food, nursed soldiers, cleaned clothes, and spent hours grinding corn for tortillas and other foods.

In the United States, it was not considered proper for women to take an active role in politics beyond supporting their husbands' ambitions. Two exceptions were journalist Margaret Fuller, who condemned the war in her articles and spent most of the war in Europe. Journalist Jane Storm supported U.S. expansion and spent much of the war in Mexico working to achieve her goals.

Women in the United States made and sent supplies to the army and wrote thousands of letters to the soldiers. They handled businesses and chores usually done by men in their family. When their husbands died in Mexico or returned unable to work, these women and their children often suffered in poverty.

Called the Heroine of Tampico, Ann McClarmonde Chase was the wife of Franklin Chase, the U.S. consul at Tampico, Mexico. Although her husband and other Americans had to leave the city after war was declared, Chase claimed British citizenship and stayed behind to manage U.S. business interests. She also gave important military information to British naval officers to pass along to the U.S. fleet.

Many upper-class Mexican women had great economic power. These included widows who owned large rancheros (ranches) in California and New Mexico. Some of these women sold horses to the U.S. military. The most remembered Mexican woman, however, was likely a peasant. She was the Maid of Monterrey and might have been several women whose courageous, compassionate actions blended into a single tale. One soldier recalled a Mexican woman who cared for the wounded of both armies during the battle of Monterrey.

> I saw her lift the head of one poor fellow, give him water, and then take her handkerchief from her own head and bind up his wounds. . . . I heard the crack of one or two guns and she, poor creature, fell. . . . She was dead!
> I turned my eyes to heaven and thought, "Oh God, and this is war!"

MINORITIES IN THE MEXICAN-AMERICAN WAR

African Americans served in the U.S. Revolutionary War (1775–1783) but were discouraged from staying in the armed forces after the War of 1812 was over. In 1820 the U.S. Army banned recruitment of any "Negro or mulatto [person of mixed black and white ancestry]," and in 1834, the last group of African American soldiers, the New Orleans Free Men of Color, was abolished. Only the U.S. Navy continued to recruit blacks.

African Americans continued to serve in the navy, particularly in positions not wanted by whites. However, economic hard times in the late 1830s drove more whites to become sailors. In 1839 the navy restricted recruitment of blacks to 5 percent of the new sailors recruited each month. That limit remained in place throughout the Mexican-American War. In 1842 the state of South Carolina created its own rule, which was in effect during the war. Any black sailor who stepped ashore in that state could be sent to jail.

The major role of the U.S. Navy in the war with Mexico was to blockade Mexico's coastal waters and rivers to prevent arms and supplies from entering the country. The sailors rarely took part in battle, but they had to face tropical heat and diseases and endless days with little to do. As fewer white sailors reenlisted, the navy came to depend on African Americans. About 1,000 African American sailors joined 7,000 whites serving in the navy during the Mexican-American War. Some naval officers thought that blacks were naturally immune to yellow fever, malaria, and other diseases because of their African ancestry. Unfortunately, black sailors were just as likely to become ill as the sick white sailors they were sent to replace.

Native Americans in Mexico were drafted into Mexico's army. They received little training and were thought of with contempt by the upper-class officers.

U.S. lieutenant colonel Ethan Allen Hitchcock recruited Manuel Dominguez, supposedly a bandit chief and native of Puebla, to organize the Mexican Spy Company. Dominguez and his men gathered information for General Winfield Scott about Mexican troop movements and road conditions from the spring of 1847 until July 1848. Each of the spies was paid $20 a month. After the war, Dominguez settled in New Orleans. Hitchcock tried to get Congress to give Dominguez a retirement salary but failed.

Beach met up with Scott not far from Veracruz and asked about Jane Storm and the "woman's revolution." Scott told him: "Never send messages of such importance by a plenipotentiary [person acting on behalf of a government] in petticoats."

Meanwhile, Storm slipped through enemy lines and stayed with supporters near Mexico City.

President Polk thought that the war was almost over. New Mexico and Alta (upper) California were relatively quiet. In late March and early April, the U.S. Navy occupied cities in Mexican Baja (lower) California. Polk appointed Nicholas Trist, a State Department official who had served as U.S. consul in Cuba and was fluent in Spanish, to accompany Scott and present treaty terms to Santa Anna. The peace representative was finally on his way.

The treaty terms Trist was authorized to negotiate were similar to those in the earlier peace plan. But Santa Anna no longer seemed ready to negotiate—that is, assuming he ever had been. The Mexican Congress declared Pedro María Anaya substitute president while Santa Anna prepared troops to stop Scott's forces. Scott continued his march to Mexico City.

6 MARCH TO MEXICO CITY

Once again, Colonel Doniphan waited for word from General Wool. This time, Doniphan's troops were in Chihuahua. Most of the men were volunteers who had signed up in June 1846 for one year of military service. In late March 1847, Doniphan had written to Wool asking when, where, and how his men could receive their pay and go home.

Some men in General Scott's command were also one-year volunteers, and Scott was eager to bring the war to a close before they left. After getting fresh horses and leaving a small force in Veracruz, Scott joined the rest of his troops as they marched toward Mexico City on the National Highway. Santa Anna and his troops were determined to stop them at Cerro Gordo, the first high hill after the swamps and coastal plains.

A half mile from Cerro Gordo was a lower hill called La Atalaya. The two hills formed a steep, narrow canyon that the Mexican troops had fortified with about 35 cannons. Scott decided that a frontal attack on the Mexicans would cost too many lives. So on April 15, Captain Robert E. Lee and Lieutenant Pierre G. T. Beauregard scouted the area. To the right of the Mexican line was a river (Rio del Plan) and perpendicular rock too steep to climb. On the left of the Mexican line were ravines that seemed impassable as well. It was on this left flank (side), near La Atalaya, that

Captain Lee faced a long day trapped under a fallen tree.

Guns and men blanketed the top of Cerro Gordo. La Atalaya remained unmanned on the left flank because Santa Anna decided that the hill was too steep for anyone to climb. Two of Santa Anna's engineers warned him that La Atalaya should be fortified, but he would not listen. Lee convinced Scott that it would be possible to get around the enemy's thin defense line near La Atalaya and then climb La Atalaya and control the main road. Lee thought that although La Atalaya was too steep for horses and oxen, it was not too steep for men.

Mexican artillery shelled U.S. soldiers moving toward La Atalaya and caused heavy losses but could not stop them. During the night, Lee showed the soldiers how to drag three heavy cannons up the hill. Team after team worked in the steady rain, hauling up pieces of cannon by rope. At dawn on April 18, the U.S. cannons on the top of La Atalaya opened fire. Meanwhile a diversionary force (other troops sent out to attract attention away from the cannons) charged the Mexicans along the main road.

The Mexican guns on Cerro Gordo had to fight an attack from two directions.

Scott's troops then charged down La Atalaya and struggled up Cerro Gordo. They captured the Mexican artillery there and used it to fire on retreating enemy troops. Another force attacked the Mexicans from the rear. Santa Anna barely escaped, while U.S. forces captured more than 3,000 officers and men.

Scott destroyed all the weapons at Cerro Gordo that he could not use. He invaded Santa Anna's nearby hacienda and took about $11,000 intended for military supplies. Scott wrote to President Polk that "Mexico . . . no longer has an army." He was wrong.

WAR AND PEACE

At about the time Scott's men buried their dead comrades at Cerro Gordo, word finally reached Colonel Doniphan to join Wool's forces at Buena Vista and prepare for the journey home. Some of the merchants on the wagon train Doniphan had escorted to Chihuahua decided to stay there. Others followed Doniphan's troops to the coast.

Lost Leg

At the Battle of Cerro Gordo, Mexican commander Antonio López de Santa Anna was forced to abandon his mule-drawn carriage and flee the battlefield on the back of a mule. Santa Anna had a wooden leg, and according to one story, he left the leg in the carriage. The following winter, Barnum's Museum in New York City advertised Santa Anna's wooden leg as its main attraction.

Santa Anna flees the Battle of Cerro Gordo.

War Correspondents

U.S. journalists covered the war with Mexico for newspapers and magazines, but only one journalist—Jane Storm—left the safety of U.S. troops and reported from behind enemy lines. The Mexican-American War was the first war to be photographed. War correspondents used a new photographic process called daguerreotype.

Dragoon Bazaleel W. Armstrong, age 32, posed for this daguerreotype in 1845.

On May 6, Nicholas Trist arrived in Veracruz with Polk's sealed proposal to end the war. Instead of delivering the proposal to General Scott personally, Trist sent it by messenger with instructions for Scott to pass the proposal to Mexican officials. Scott refused. He didn't know what was in the proposal, and he thought an armistice should be negotiated between military commanders, not civilians. Scott also refused to meet with Trist about a week later.

Meanwhile, Moses Beach and his daughter had made it safely to New Orleans. The U.S. government paid Beach $2,609.05 for his expenses, and on May 11, Beach met with President Polk. Jane Storm made her way to New York City via Havana, Cuba, then met with Polk on May 13.

Shortly after the battle of Cerro Gordo, Scott released about 3,700 one-year volunteers. Their terms were about up, and Scott wanted them to get transportation home before yellow fever season was in full swing. At about the same time, Doniphan's troops made it to Buena Vista. They were released from duty, marched to the east coast of Mexico, and sailed to New Orleans. Since leaving Missouri, Doniphan's regiment had trekked about 3,500 miles, inspiring the U.S. public to remember their long march in story and song.

Scott continued up the National Highway toward Mexico City. Santa Anna withdrew his troops, planning to take a stand closer to the capital. So with little difficulty, Scott's forces reached Puebla, a large city surrounded by volcanoes. Scott set up his headquarters there in May, less than 100 miles from Mexico City.

The occupation of Puebla, which would last

> **EYEWITNESS QUOTE:**
> **U.S. TROOPS IN PUEBLA**
>
> "I gave in to curiosity, and went to meet our future masters. . . . I saw a hundred harrowed-looking men whose uniforms were poor and inelegant . . . feeble, skinny, even crippled men . . . everything that bad taste and stinginess can produce of the ridiculous, sordid, and gross."
>
> —Puebla resident, May 1847

for about three months, was an uneasy one. Many of the city's 60,000 residents were hostile to Scott's men. Guerrilla units attacked the troops and supply lines.

GUERRILLAS

Derived from a Spanish word meaning "little war," guerrillas are people who are not usually part of a regular army. They attack small groups of enemy troops and destroy their supplies.

However, Scott tried to show the people of Puebla that he had come to "liberate" them from an oppressive government. Scott insisted that high-ranking U.S. officers attend Catholic Mass in full-dress uniform and that U.S. soldiers salute priests. Scott's military bands played dance music in the plaza (square) every afternoon.

In late June, Nicholas Trist came down with a bad case of dysentery. General Scott sent him a jar of jelly made with guava, a kind of tropical fruit, which was thought to soothe the intestines. Soon the two men developed what was to be a lasting friendship. Trist had given Polk's peace proposal to a British diplomat to deliver.

Santa Anna no longer had the power to negotiate, because the Mexican Congress made it a crime to deal with the United States. Even so, he let it be known that money might change the minds of Mexican officials and bring about negotiations. Trist gave Santa Anna $10,000, which Scott borrowed from funds he had available to pay for secret service activities, but there was no movement toward peace. One confidential (secret) source told Trist,

who informed Polk and Scott, that Santa Anna would not make peace until U.S. troops approached Mexico City. Santa Anna would only weakly defend the city and then ask for a truce.

With the one-year volunteers gone, Scott reported that he had 2,000 sick soldiers and 8,000 men who could fight. In early August, 2,000 fresh troops landed in Veracruz and moved as fast as possible through yellow fever swamps to Puebla. Then Scott, most of his troops, and a long train of wagons left Puebla. After three days' travel through mountain passes, they reached the Valley of Mexico. In the center of the valley rose the fortified walls of the nation's capital.

MEXICO CITY

The Valley of Mexico is a marshy basin about 120 miles around, with lakes and lava fields in it. The few roads into Mexico City were heavily guarded. Santa Anna asked all men aged 15 to 60 to defend the city. About 7,000 Mexican troops awaited Scott's forces at El Peñón, a large hill near the main road to the city—in Santa Anna's opinion, the only road U.S. troops could take.

Scott's scouts found a muddy path that was barely passable, but it allowed U.S. troops to avoid El Peñón and approach to within a few miles of Mexico City from a different direction. When they saw Scott's troops so close, many residents fled the capital.

About 20,000 Mexican troops gathered near the Churubusco River, in a convent with barricades and along a heavily fortified bridgehead (end of a bridge nearest an enemy). Again Santa Anna thought that the rocky terrain would force U.S. troops to wage a frontal attack.

MEDICAL CARE

"The dark cloud of disease hovered over us," wrote one military surgeon traveling to Mexico in the 1840s. In the war with Mexico, about nine times as many U.S. soldiers died from disease as from battle. Death from disease among the soldiers was ten times greater than that of civilians in the United States.

Doctors vaccinated soldiers for smallpox to prevent epidemics of this disease. But General Winfield Scott worried about yellow fever, which was easy to catch in the summer. He planned his attack on Veracruz to avoid yellow fever. Luckily, yellow fever that year was not as dangerous as Scott feared it might be. The overall death rate from the disease for that spring and summer was about 28 percent (about 1 out of every 4 soldiers), which was less than the 33 percent (1 out of 3 soldiers) death rate for patients hospitalized with diarrhea or dysentery.

Doctors used quinine, made from the bark of a tropical tree, to reduce the high fever in yellow fever and malaria. Other less effective and sometimes harmful treatments were baths, mustard plasters, mercury compounds (such as calomel) for "free evacuation of the bowels," and cupping (drawing blood to the surface of the skin by creating a vacuum). Some soldiers carried their own supply of opium to ease pain.

Amputations were common. Surgeon General Thomas Lawson used ether for the first time in Veracruz to put a soldier to sleep before he amputated his leg. Ether was first used in experiments at Massachusetts General Hospital in October 1846. A civilian physician brought ether to Mexico and demonstrated its use. But Lawson thought the explosive chemical and fragile equipment were not practical for military operations there. Another surgeon thought ether slowed healing and led to infection and bleeding. So the medical corps (military medical unit) did not use much ether in the Mexican-American War.

U.S. military hospitals were set up in churches and monastery buildings. The largest was at Veracruz, which also served as a supply depot. Field hospitals were built along the battle route. The army had few military physicians, and surgeons had huge workloads. Some volunteer doctors were incompetent or unreliable. Surgeon General Lawson traveled with the soldiers in Scott's campaign and provided good medical care.

The average soldier had two hospital stays for wounds or disease during his tour of duty. Hospitals were often overcrowded and understaffed. So many severely ill and wounded soldiers were sent to New Orleans that the army built a new hospital there in 1848. The soldiers headed to New Orleans had to put up with a bumpy ride by wagon to the coast, then a filthy and disease-ridden journey by ship, where there was not enough medical staff to provide for them. Many died along the way.

Nevertheless, U.S. troops received better care than Mexican troops, who had no medical corps. Mexican soldiers were often cared for by families and friends, and even slight wounds could prove fatal.

In August 1847, Scott's troops prepare to cross the marshy basin surrounding Mexico City.

Again Scott looked for a way around enemy lines. This time, U.S. troops would have to cross the Pedregal, which one soldier described as "hell with the fires out." Rutted with deep gullies, the Pedregal was roughly a five-mile-wide circle of hardened lava sharp enough to shred horse hooves.

Captain Lee, Lieutenant Beauregard, and a scouting party ventured into the lava bed. Fortunately, they skirmished with Mexicans, who retreated, revealing a hidden path through the Pedregal. The next

Kirby Smith

The night before attacking Mexico City, Captain Kirby Smith wrote to his wife, "I almost despair when I reflect upon the destitute situation in which you will be left, with the three children . . . should I fall in the coming battle. . . . Tomorrow will be a day of slaughter." The next day, Smith died.

day, Scott sent out 500 soldiers to widen the path. They came under attack too.

Scott wanted to use the same tactic that worked at Cerro Gordo—a diversionary frontal attack and a surprise attack from behind enemy lines. Scott's main headquarters was on the side of the lava bed closest to Churubusco, while another force, led by Persifor Smith, was on the other side, near the town of Contreras. Smith decided to attack a position in the enemy lines there. He wanted to alert Scott and ask for a diversionary attack. So that night in a heavy rainstorm, Captain Lee crossed the lava bed, which was lit only by flashes of lightning. After meeting with Scott, Lee led a group of soldiers back through the Pedregal to aid Smith the next morning.

As the sun rose on August 20, U.S. troops attacked. Mexican forces near Contreras were surprised and fled toward the road leading to Churubusco. At the same time, Scott's main force attacked Churubusco from the opposite side. During

A U.S. dragoon pursues a Mexican cavalryman in the Battle of Churubusco in August 1847.

the fierce battle, Scott's men captured 72 deserters in the San Patricio Battalion, along with their leader, Captain John Riley, and held them for court-martial (military trial). Finally, the Mexican soldiers retreated, and Scott ordered his men to rest.

Deserters

According to official military records, at least 4,000 men deserted the U.S. armed services during each year of the war with Mexico. Mexican commanders encouraged Catholics in the U.S. Army to support their fellow Catholics in Mexico. Propaganda pamphlets smuggled into U.S. camps read: "Throw away your arms and run to us." However, most deserters left for reasons that were not related to religion. They were often ill or maimed, sick of bad food and poor living conditions, uneasy about fighting in a foreign country that hadn't threatened the United States, or just plain homesick.

Captain Lee was made a lieutenant colonel for his actions in the battles of Contreras and Churubusco. Scott wrote that Lee's crossing of the Pedregal was "the greatest feat [act] of physical and moral courage performed by any individual" in the Mexican campaign and that Lee was "the very best soldier I ever saw in the field."

The next day, Santa Anna sent a message to Scott asking for an armistice and a chance to negotiate a peace treaty. Scott agreed. But the negotiations stalled, particularly over the southern boundary of Texas. At first, Trist, who was in Mexico City, was willing to make the Nueces River the southern border but then realized his mistake. President Polk needed to have the Rio Grande as the border in order to justify that "American blood" had been shed on "American soil." The disputed territory between the Nueces River and the Rio Grande seemed too important an issue for either side to give up. On September 6, Scott threatened to start fighting again if

Many soldiers died when the U.S. Army destroyed the metal foundry at Molino del Rey.

Santa Anna did not come to an agreement by noon the next day. Santa Anna refused.

On September 8, U.S. forces attacked a metal foundry near a mill compound called Molino del Rey. Scott had heard that the foundry turned church bells into cannons, but that information proved to be false. Scott's forces won the battle but at a high cost in lives on both sides.

Santa Anna's forces withdrew to defend Mexico City, while Scott's forces made their way toward the capital from the west. Guarding the city's western gate was the Castle of Chapultepec, a summer palace that had become a military academy similar to West Point. Chapultepec stood on the top of a rocky hill about 200 feet above the city. Scott decided to capture the castle to make sure his troops would not be attacked from the rear. Scott's soldiers called the Castle of Chapultepec the Halls of the Montezumas. Inside, however, there were only about 800 soldiers, including 80 military cadets. Their commander, Nicolás Bravo, had asked for reinforcements but had received none.

On September 12, Scott's men blasted the castle walls with artillery. The following day, the soldiers climbed the castle and defeated its defenders. According to legend, the bravest defenders were the cadets (students)—the Niños Héroes—boy

> **EYEWITNESS QUOTE:**
> **MEXICO CITY AFTER WAR**
>
> "The mere sight of the deserted city inspired sorrow and fear. It resembled beauty without life, the naked bones of a skull where lovely eyes had sparkled."
>
> —*Apuntes para la Historia de la Guerra*, a book written by 15 Mexican soldiers after the war

heroes. Six of them were said to have committed suicide rather than surrender. One cadet, Juan Escutia, wrapped himself in the Mexican flag and jumped from the castle walls.

When the battle was over, Scott's forces fought their way to the city gates. By then only about 6,000 of Scott's exhausted soldiers could have faced another day of fighting. That night Mexican political leaders met with Santa Anna. At 4:00 A.M., they went to Scott's headquarters and surrendered Mexico City. Later that morning, U.S. forces marched into the capital, while military bands played "Hail, Columbia," "Washington's March," "Yankee Doodle," and "Hail to the Chief." By day's end, the Stars and Stripes flew over Mexico's national palace.

Save My Brother

The night before U.S. troops were expected to attack the military academy at Chapultepec, Mexican lieutenant colonel Juan Cano gave his brother Lorenzo a sealed message to take to their uncle. Lorenzo thought the message had to do with getting supplies to Mexico's army. The message really read: "Dear Uncle, I am certain that tomorrow we will die, and because I don't want to give my elderly parents the unbearable bitterness of receiving news of the death of two sons at the same time, I beg you to keep my brother Lorenzo from returning to my side, as I am sure that he would die with me if he remained at Chapultepec." Lorenzo stayed and Juan died.

U.S. troops storm the Castle of Chapultepec on a hill in Mexico City in September 1847, leading to victory for the United States in the war against Mexico.

THE STRUGGLE FOR PEACE

Despite the blare of "Yankee Doodle" from Scott's military band, not much was dandy. Mobs of angry Mexicans threatened the U.S. troops who entered their capital on September 14, 1847. Scott announced martial law and appointed Major General John Quitman, a Mississippi politician and land speculator in Texas, the city's governor. Scott warned that his soldiers would tear down a whole block of buildings in any place where there was sniper fire. Scott also called for a $3 million tax on Mexico to pay for upkeep of U.S. soldiers on Mexican territory. President Polk approved of the tax as a way to avoid forcing U.S. taxpayers—and voters—to pay for the unpopular war.

Santa Anna left the capital and resigned the presidency. Manuel de la Peña y Peña, the head of Mexico's Supreme Court, became interim president. He moved to Querétaro, about 170 miles northwest of Mexico City, and struggled to form and maintain a government there. Meanwhile, Santa Anna gathered a few thousand volunteers and surrounded the U.S. forces at Puebla.

On October 11, Santa Anna learned that Peña y Peña had ordered him court-martialed. Santa Anna fled to Jamaica, and the siege of Puebla came to an end. Afterward, conditions in Mexico City were fairly stable. The Mexican Congress assembled in Querétaro. On November 11,

Diplomat Nicholas Trist (right) disobeyed a presidential order and negotiated peace with Mexico.

Pedro María Anaya was elected interim president. A few days later, delegates from seven Mexican states voted for peace.

On November 16, just as Nicholas Trist prepared to negotiate a treaty, he received a letter dated October 6 from Secretary of State James Buchanan. Buchanan wrote that the president "has directed me to recall you from your mission. . . . He has determined not to make another offer to . . . the Mexican government. . . . They must now sue for peace."

Trist began to arrange for his departure. Scott told him that the first available escort to Veracruz would be on December 4. In the meantime, Scott, Peña y Peña, and others pressured Trist to stay and negotiate an end to the war. Trist decided to disobey orders from the president. On December 4, he wrote to Polk and explained that if the present "opportunity be not seized at once, all chance of making a treaty at all will be lost . . . probably forever."

When he received Trist's response, Polk was furious. The previous April, Polk and Buchanan had discussed the possibility that Moses Y. Beach, their confidential agent, might come up with a treaty giving Polk the territories he wanted. Polk wrote that he would take Beach's treaty to the Senate, noting that it "will be a good joke . . . and take the whole country by sur-

prise." But Trist had politely but deliberately disobeyed Polk, and the president felt that the war was slipping out of his control.

In December Congress continued to argue over slavery and the possible outcomes of the war with Mexico. On December 22, a newly elected Whig congressman named Abraham Lincoln stood in the House of Representatives and vigorously opposed the war. In a document called the "Spot Resolution," Lincoln noted that the spot where Polk claimed U.S. blood had been shed was in disputed territory and arguably a part of Mexico.

The new year began with fresh troops from the United States arriving in Mexico and California. Despite restlessness among troops who had been fighting longer and wanted to go home, Mexico City remained fairly peaceful. Scott and the religious leader of Mexico City, Juan Manual, had even worked out a release program for captured Mexican soldiers.

On January 2, 1848, Mexican treaty commissioners had their first formal meeting with Nicholas Trist. Treaty negotiations continued for three weeks. Trist was a tough negotiator, but he did allow Mexico to keep Baja California, as well as land connecting that peninsula with the rest of Mexico. Anaya's term as interim president ended and Peña y Peña took office again. There were tensions between political groups that supported peace with the United States and those that wanted to continue the war at all cost. The new president worried that his government might fall apart before a treaty could be signed.

Tensions that had been simmering for months between General Scott and some of his officers, particularly Gideon Pillow, finally boiled over. General Pillow, who was second in command under Scott, was a former law partner of President Polk and a Democrat. According to Scott, who was eager to be a presidential candidate for the Whig Party, Pillow did not act with the high moral standards that military duty demanded, and he took credit for victories he had little part in achieving. Pillow thought Scott boastful and, under an assumed name, published criticisms of his conduct in U.S. newspapers.

President Polk ordered an investigation of the dispute in Mexico City between Scott and those serving under him. Scott was relieved of command during this time, caught yellow fever on the way back to the United States, and nearly died. General Kearny, who had become military governor, first of Veracruz and then of Mexico City, also fell ill with yellow fever. He returned to Washington and died soon after.

The news in Washington that January was about John Frémont, the son-in-law of Senator Benton. Frémont had been charged by General Kearny, his former friend, of mutiny and disobeying orders concerning who was to be governor of California during the fighting there. Despite Benton's best efforts, the charges had not been dropped, and Frémont faced a court-martial. He was convicted and sentenced to resign his commission. President Polk later overturned the conviction, but Frémont resigned anyway.

But the really big news came on January 24, 1848. While building a new sawmill for John Sutter in California, John Marshall discovered gold!

GOLD MINE FOUND.—In the newly made raceway of the Saw Mill recently erected by Captain Sutter, on the American Fork, gold has been found in considerable quantities. One person brought thirty dollars worth to New Helvetia, gathered there in a short time. California, no doubt, is rich in mineral wealth; great chances here for scientific capitalists. Gold has been found in almost every part of the country.

This ad ran in the San Francisco *Californian* on March 5, 1848. The discovery of gold brought thousands of gold seekers to California.

THE ENEMY'S POINT OF VIEW

Soon after Mexico won independence from Spain in 1821, rebellions broke out in the vast territory that Mexico formally owned but barely controlled. Mexico's army spent more time fighting Mexicans between 1821 and 1854 than it did fighting troops from the United States. Still, the invasion of Mexican territory and two years of war with the United States was more devastating to Mexico than the various civil wars in the early years of Mexico's independence.

Texas had declared itself an independent republic a decade before the Mexican-American War and wanted to join the United States. The inhabitants of California and New Mexico had few ties with the central government in Mexico City. Their response to an invasion of U.S. forces ranged from open hostility and sad resignation to approval. Most Mexicans who lived south of the Rio Grande were deeply opposed to U.S. forces in their country.

From the Mexican point of view, the United States wanted to satisfy its own greed for more land and resources, and it was determined to get that land by any means necessary. The invasion of Mexico and the unfair postwar treatment of Mexican Americans in California, Texas, and the American Southwest has left a bitter taste among Mexicans and Mexican Americans that lingers to this day.

U.S. troops, under the command of General Winfield Scott, ride into Mexico City's central square to seize power after the Mexican-American War.

THE TREATY OF GUADALUPE HIDALGO

The treaty commissioners met in Guadalupe Hidalgo on February 2, 1848. Not knowing about Marshall's discovery, they signed a treaty giving California's goldfields to the United States. Then they celebrated Mass at the Basilica of the Virgin of Guadalupe.

Written in English and Spanish, the lengthy treaty contained 23 separate articles (main points) and referred to other official agreements between the United States and Mexico. The treaty's major points required the United States to:

- Evacuate all forces from Mexico within three months (Article IV)
- Prevent Native American raids into Mexico (Article XI)
- Pay $15 million to Mexico, with $3 million paid immediately and the remaining $12 million in four annual installments at 6 percent interest (Article XII)
- Pay for damage claims against Mexico under two previous agreements (in 1839 and 1843) and all financial obligations of U.S. citizens to Mexico, not to exceed $3.25 million (Articles XIII and XV)
- Receive from Mexico all territory north of the Rio Grande and across the Colorado River to the Pacific Ocean (Article V)

The ceded (surrendered) land was about half of Mexico's territory, including what is California, New Mexico, Nevada, Utah, Texas, most of Arizona, and parts of Colorado and Wyoming. Mexicans living in the ceded territory had one year in which to choose their citizenship. If they chose to remain in the United States, they would become U.S. citizens with all the rights of citizenship, including religious freedom and enjoyment of liberty and property (Articles VIII and IX). About 2,000 Mexicans moved south of the Rio Grande to keep their Mexican citizenship. Nearly 80,000 Mexicans remained in the United States. For all its details, the treaty failed to mention specifically the rights of more than 200,000 native peoples who lived in the ceded territory and who had been granted full rights of citizenship under Mexican law.

The Treaty of Guadalupe Hidalgo reached the White House on February 19, more than a week after President Polk had learned of gold in California. Polk found the treaty terms acceptable, although he still was angry with Nicholas Trist for disobeying his recall order. Changing nothing, Polk gave the treaty to the Senate to vote on. There, like the Wilmot Proviso, the treaty soon became a lightning rod for disagreement and debate.

John Quincy Adams

Just before President Polk submitted the peace treaty to the Senate, congressman and former president John Quincy Adams suffered a stroke in the House of Representatives and died two days later. Several months earlier, on January 3, 1848, Adams and others had asked the House of Representatives to declare that the war with Mexico was unconstitutional and to call for immediate withdrawal of U.S. forces.

This mural in Los Angeles pictures Mexican and U.S. negotiators signing the Treaty of Guadalupe Hidalgo, ending the Mexican-American War.

Some senators urged the United States not to take any land from Mexico. Others said that the laws of war and occupation allowed the United States to take all of Mexico. Debates took place about Trist's authority and arguments over slavery in the new territory.

On March 10, however, the Senate approved an amended version of the treaty by a 38-to-14 vote. President Polk signed the treaty on March 16. Senator Ambrose Sevier and Attorney General Nathan Clifford delivered the treaty to the Mexican government.

The Mexican Congress was also divided. Many were appalled at the loss of so much territory. A large minority favored a return to war. Peña y Peña urged the Congress to accept the treaty as a way to end the nation's suffering. Treaty commissioner Bernardo Couto voiced a different perspective. He said: "The present treaty . . . serves to recover that better part of that which is already under the control of the conquering army of the United States; it is more exactly an agreement of recovery than an agreement of cession." On May 30, the Mexican Congress approved the U.S. version of the treaty.

On June 12, the U.S. flag was taken down from the National Palace in Mexico City, and the Mexican flag rose it its place. The ratified treaty arrived in Washington, D.C., from Mexico on July 4. Polk officially proclaimed peace between Mexico and the United States on Independence Day.

> **EYEWITNESS QUOTE:**
> **LOSS**
>
> "The truth is that a fertile and beautiful part of our territory is being ceded. . . . I have no wish to obscure the truth, much less to deny the pain I feel at the separation from the Mexicans of California and New Mexico."
>
> —Manuel de la Peña y Peña

Shame

Virginia Trist, whose husband Nicholas negotiated the Treaty of Guadalupe Hidalgo, said that when Mexican treaty commissioner Bernardo Couto was about to sign, he said to her husband, "This must be a proud moment for you—no less proud for you than it is humiliating for us." Nicholas Trist was said to have replied, "[W]e are making peace, let that be our only thought." But she said Trist later explained to her: "Could these Mexicans have seen into my heart at that moment, they would have known that my feeling of shame as an American was far stronger than theirs could be."

A CHANGING UNITED STATES

Change was coming fast to the United States. A convention that began on July 3, 1848, in Seneca Falls, New York, marked the official start of the women's rights movement in the United States.

The U.S. presidential election was coming up that November. Because Polk decided, after all, to serve only one term, Democrats picked Michigan senator Lewis Cass as their presidential candidate. Since the last election, Iowa and Wisconsin had entered the United States as free (nonslave) states. A group strongly supporting the abolition of slavery started the Free Soil Party. Their candidate was former president Martin Van Buren.

The Whig Party wanted a war hero as their candidate, even though many Whigs had opposed the war. The war might not be popular, but war heroes were. Winfield Scott was interested in running, but Whig Party members worried about the ongoing investigation involving Pillow and others. So they picked the older, more colorful hero Zachary Taylor. Taylor won the three-way race.

In 1849 California was invaded by the "forty-niners." That year as many as 90,000 people came to California from all over the globe. They all hoped to get rich from mining gold or selling to gold miners. Gold was easy to find on the surface then (by 1852 most of the surface deposits were gone), and thousands of prospectors panned for the precious metal in rivers and streams.

A prosperous United States from the Atlantic to the Pacific was just what Polk had in mind when he decided to acquire much of Mexico. The California gold rush made the state wealthy and was a powerful reason for settlers to decide to "go West."

Polk attended the inauguration of 64-year-old Zachary Taylor on March 5, 1849, then retired to Tennessee. Four exhausting years at the White House had left him in poor health. On June 15, James Polk died of the disease cholera at age 53, three months after leaving office.

TWO NATIONS, ONE BORDER

8

The Mexican-American War killed a large number of people. As many as 25,000 Mexican soldiers died in battle, and an unknown number of civilians died as a result of the war. Of the more than 104,000 U.S. soldiers who went to war (about 30,000 regulars and 74,000 volunteers), about 1,500 were killed in action. Another 12,000 men died from accidents or disease, not including soldiers who later died at home from diseases caught while in service.

After the war, political groups in Mexico argued about how to live in the shadow of El Coloso del Norte (the Colossus of the North, or the United States). Some thought that the best way to resist further expansion by the United States was to bring back a monarchy and strengthen ties with Europe. Others thought that Mexico should create a political and economic system similar to that in the United States. Neither José Joaquín Herrera, who returned to power after the war, nor Mariano Arista, who replaced him in 1851, could restore stability.

In 1853 Antonio López de Santa Anna once again returned from exile and rose to power in a military coup (takeover). He met with James Gadsden, who was sent by the United States to settle territorial disputes that were the results of the Treaty of Guadalupe Hidalgo and to purchase land. Santa Anna wanted more money. Gadsden had a deal.

As signed into law in 1854, the Gadsden Purchase Treaty gave the United States

The United States
after the
Mexican-American
War, 1853

- - - - - Current state
borders

about 30,000 square miles of territory south of the Gila River, including Tucson, Arizona, and land suitable for a railroad line. In return, Mexico got $10 million. Under the treaty, the United States also paid Mexico $5 million for damages from the raids of native peoples on Mexico. It also canceled Article XI of the Treaty of Guadalupe Hidalgo, which made the United States pay Mexico for damage on Mexican soil by native peoples living in U.S. territory. The Gadsden Treaty did not change the promise under the Treaty of Guadalupe Hidalgo that former Mexican citizens in the ceded territory would have all the rights of U.S. citizens. But the United States put Native Americans on reservations and did not grant them full citizenship until the 1930s.

Many former Mexicans in the ceded territory faced discrimination by their American neighbors and sometimes faced physical violence. The Federal Land Grant of 1851 stated that prewar Mexicans who owned land had to submit papers within two years or the land would be turned over to the U.S. government. Since Mexico's system of land ownership wasn't always written, many Mexican Americans could not prove they owned the land and houses they had lived in for generations.

Californios were overwhelmed as the gold rush brought 200,000 people to California within three years. Not all Californios suffered as a result. Pío Pico, who had fled to Mexico after he lost the governorship of the Los Angeles region

Former Californio Pío Pico returned to California after the war. He is pictured here with his wife.

Eagle Pass; or Life on the Border described the hardships of Mexican Americans living near the Rio Grande. The book was published in 1852, the same year as *Uncle Tom's Cabin,* Harriet Beecher Stowe's famous novel about slavery. *Eagle Pass* was written by Cora Montgomery, which was the pen name of Jane Storm. Storm had married businessman William Cazneau in 1849, after her failed diplomatic adventures in Mexico. She had moved to his ranch in Texas near the United States-Mexico border.

GAINS AND LOSSES

With its huge increase in land, the United States gained the natural resources—including gold in California—that Mexico lost. Explorers mapped the new land and established transportation routes linking the Pacific Coast with the industries of the Northeast and Midwest. The United States grew rapidly after the war as immigrants flooded in from around the globe. The United States had 23,191,867 citizens in 1850, about 10 million more people than lived in Mexico. More people meant more consumers, larger markets, and more cheap labor. Levi Strauss picked the right time and place when he created his first pair of work pants in California in 1850. U.S. industries that prospered during the war continued to thrive. For many people, from the small business owner to wealthy owners of large businesses, Manifest Destiny meant a prosperous future.

during the war, returned to California and reclaimed his land. He became a wealthy businessman and served on the Los Angeles City Council.

After 1852, however, most Mexican Americans were denied the right to mine in northern California. The state's Supreme Court declared that water belongs to individuals rather than to the community. This ruling ignored the fact that water was shared by native peoples and many Mexicans. Anglos dammed streams, made claims to mines, and built fences. Hundreds of Mexican Americans sued for their rights and property, but few won their cases. Mexican Americans lost their mines, their farms, and their ranches—and their livelihood.

But prosperity could not hide social and political problems. In 1849 conservatives created the American Party. Since their reply to questions about party policies was "I don't know," the party became known as the Know-Nothings. Party members opposed the Catholic Church, immigration, and allowing foreign-born people to hold political office.

President Taylor died suddenly on July 9, 1850, leaving the nation in the hands of

President Millard Fillmore

Vice President Millard Fillmore. A New York lawyer who grew up poor, Fillmore was determined to prevent slavery from tearing the United States apart. As a way to ease tensions, he supported a group of laws called the Compromise of 1850 based on whether to allow slavery in the lands acquired from Mexico.

One part of the Compromise of 1850 involved Texas. As the Lone Star Republic, Texas had claimed land extending the entire length of the Rio Grande, including territory well beyond the boundaries of the Mexican state of Texas. After the Mexican-American War, Texans tried to organize Santa Fe County in New

Mexico as part of Texas. New Mexico proposed a state constitution specifying boundaries that included land claimed by Texas. Federal troops kept the Texas Rangers out of the disputed territory while Congress investigated the dispute.

After months of debate, Congress decided to leave Texas with only about two-thirds of the territory claimed by the Lone Star Republic. Congress also gave Texas $10 million, which the state used to pay debts it had built up while a separate nation. Texas voters approved the plan, and their governor signed it into law.

As part of the Compromise of 1850, California entered the United States as a free state. The territories of New Mexico and Utah were created, and the slavery issue was left to settlers there to decide. Slave trading was finally abolished in Washington, D.C., but the Fugitive Slave Act made it a federal crime for anyone to directly or indirectly help escaping slaves. Under the new law, for example, a woman in Ohio who left food on her doorstep for escaping slaves could be

Troops called the Texas Rangers were formed to help keep order in the area that would become the state of Texas.

Escaped slaves who had made new homes in nonslave states could legally be captured and returned to their owners under the Fugitive Slave Act.

fined $1,000 and spend six months in prison. The act also established a system of rewards for slaves returned to their owners, which encouraged bounty hunters (men who were paid to hunt down and capture outlaws) to capture free blacks too and sell them to willing slave owners.

The Fugitive Slave Act angered many people, even those who had previously tolerated the southern slave system. Abolitionists became more determined to end slavery. And many African Americans, escaped slaves as well as free blacks, fled to Canada.

In 1854 Congress also passed the Kansas-Nebraska Act, which made slavery legal in territories where it had been prohibited by the Missouri Compromise in 1820. Tensions over slavery neared the breaking point. At the same time, Congress added four new regiments to the army to help protect settlers on the lands gained from Mexico. Secretary of War Jefferson Davis named Colonel Robert E. Lee to be second

in command of a cavalry regiment. The new assignment meant that for the first time in Lee's career he would formally command combat troops rather than advise commanders as a member of the engineering corps.

While political tensions over slavery threatened to divide the United States, Mexico was also on the edge of political turmoil. By agreeing to the Gadsden Purchase in 1853, President Santa Anna had once again used his power for personal gain and done little to help the Mexican people. After the purchase, which gave still more territory to the United States, Santa Anna was overthrown and fled into exile.

Gum!

During his final exile from Mexico, Antonio López de Santa Anna spent time in New York City. There he met Thomas Adams, who was trying to make tires and other products from rubber. Santa Anna chewed chicle, the hardened gum of the sapodilla tree, which grows abundantly in Mexico. Santa Anna and Adams first thought that the chicle could be mixed with rubber to improve Adams's products, but the experiments failed. When Adams saw a little girl buy paraffin wax to chew, he decided to sell Santa Anna's chicle as Adams New York Gum. The new chewing gum sold for a penny a piece starting in February 1871.

Benito Juárez led the reform movement in Mexico. He was elected president of Mexico in 1861.

But this time, Mexico started *la reforma*—a period of national reform. The reform movement in Mexico was headed by Benito Juárez, of the Zapotec people. Under his guidance, Mexico created a new constitution in 1857, which weakened the political power of the Catholic Church and brought about social reforms. Conservatives staged a revolt and invited France to put in Archduke Maximilian of Austria as emperor of Mexico. But the reformers soon returned Juárez to power and laid the basic foundations of democracy in Mexico.

While Mexico worked through its reform period, the United States erupted into a devastating civil war. In 1861 the Confederate States of America seceded from the United States. Military officers who had honed their fighting skills together in the Mexican-American War turned against each other in the bloodiest conflict in U.S. history.

General Robert E. Lee and General Ulysses S. Grant spoke about their experiences in the war with Mexico when they met at Appomattox Court House, Virginia, on April 9, 1865. General Lee then surrendered his Confederate (Southern) troops to Grant, who gave Lee's starving soldiers a day's rations and allowed them to return home. The last of the Confederate army surrendered to U.S. troops a few weeks later.

Santa Anna, against whom both generals had fought, was permitted to return to Mexico after his country's period of reform. He spent his remaining years as a private citizen, starting in 1874, and died there in 1876. Lee, however, never actually became a full U.S. citizen again during his lifetime. After the Civil War, he took the oath of allegiance to the United States that was required of Southern leaders and sent it to Washington, D.C., but the oath was lost. Lee became president of Washington College, in Lexington, Virginia, and died in 1870. The college was later renamed Washington and Lee. And 100 years after Lee's death, an employee of the National Archives found Lee's oath of allegiance. Congress restored full citizenship to Robert E. Lee in 1975.

RETURNING TO THE RIVER

During la reforma and the U.S. Civil War, flooding and erosion caused the Rio Grande to gradually shift south. Then the river made an abrupt shift southward after

U.S. president Lyndon B. Johnson and Mexican president Gustavo Díaz Orgaz *(onstage center)* met at the Chamizal National Monument *(above)* in October 1967. The two leaders signed the Chamizal treaty and commemorated the completion of the monument and channel that were agreed upon at the Chamizal Convention by Mexican president Adolfo López Mateos and U.S. president John F. Kennedy in 1963.

a flood in 1864. The shift added land to Texas that had been part of Chihuahua, Mexico, and the resentments of the 1846–1848 war flared up again.

In 1911 an international court ruled that Mexico was entitled to part of the disputed territory (called La Chamizal), but the United States did not return any land. In 1963 U.S. president John Kennedy finally agreed to a compromise, called the Chamizal Convention. After a century of bickering, the United States and Mexico agreed to share the cost of building a concrete channel to keep the Rio Grande in its pre-1864 border and to return about 630 acres of land to Mexico. In 1967 Presidents Lyndon Johnson and Gustavo Díaz Orgaz met on the border and announced the completion of the project.

The Chamizal dispute was minor compared with the boundary disputes that had touched off war between the United States and Mexico. But the shift in the Rio Grande brought an opportunity for a shift in relations between neighbors. The U.S. National Park Service marked the occasion by establishing the Chamizal National Memorial "dedicated to furthering the spirit of understanding and goodwill between two nations that share one border."

What's in a Name?

As of 2003, the official name of Mexico—the one used in the Treaty of Guadalupe Hidalgo—is Estados Unidos Mexicanos, or "United Mexican States." Some people want to change the official name to Mexico. One Mexican historian recently noted: "Maybe we should just erase 'Mexico' and keep 'United States.' That's the sad truth: we are an extension of that country."

MAJOR BATTLES OF THE MEXICAN-AMERICAN WAR

Palo Alto, Mexico	May 8, 1846
Resaca de la Palma, Mexico	May 9, 1846
Monterrey, Mexico	September 20, 1846
Buena Vista, Mexico	February 22–23, 1847
Chihuahua, Mexico	February 28, 1847
Veracruz, Mexico	March 22–26, 1847
Cerro Gordo, Mexico	April 17–18, 1847
Churubusco, Mexico	August 20, 1847
Molino del Rey, Mexico	September 8, 1847
Castle of Chapultepec, Mexico	September 12, 1847

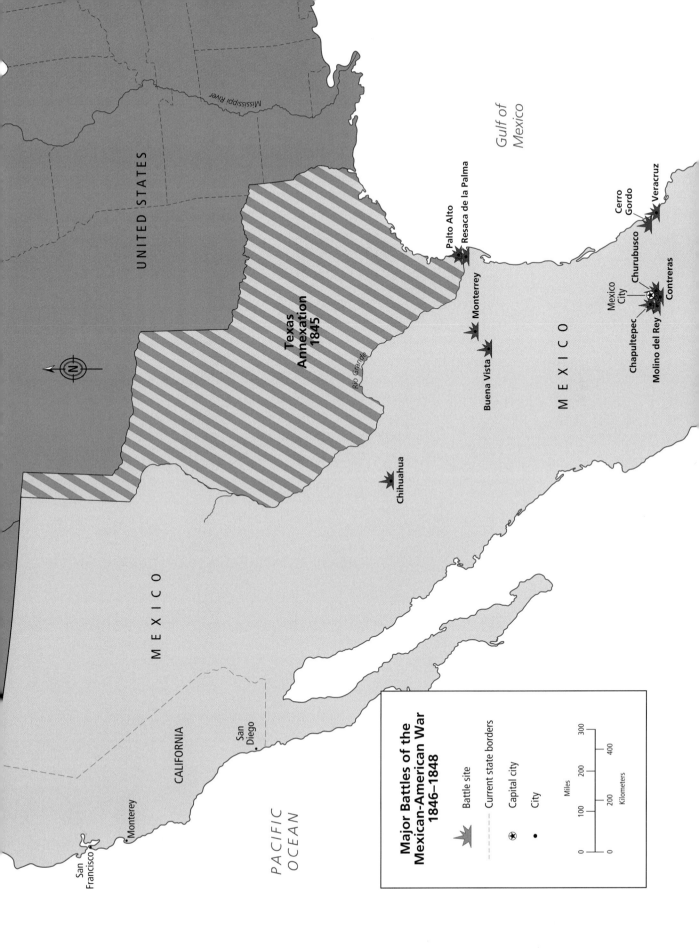

UNITED STATES

Mississippi River

Gulf of Mexico

Texas Annexation 1845

Rio Grande

Palto Alto
Resaca de la Palma

Monterrey

Cerro Gordo
Veracruz

Buena Vista

Churubusco
Mexico City
Contreras
Chapultepec
Molino del Rey

Chihuahua

M E X I C O

M E X I C O

CALIFORNIA

San Diego

Monterey

San Francisco

PACIFIC OCEAN

Major Battles of the Mexican-American War 1846–1848

✹ Battle site

- - - Current state borders

⊛ Capital city

• City

Miles

0   100   200   300

0   200   400

Kilometers

MEXICAN-AMERICAN WAR TIMELINE

1836 Texas declares independence from Mexico, becoming the Lone Star Republic.

Santa Anna captures the Alamo.

1845 Texas accepts U.S. statehood.

U.S. troops move into disputed land, July 4.

Texas admitted to the United States, December 29.

1846 Battle of Palo Alto fought May 8.

The United States declares war on Mexico.

Army of the West ordered to occupy New Mexico and California.

U.S. troops cross the Rio Grande, May 13–18.

Bear Flaggers declare California an independent republic on June 14.

U.S. forces occupy Los Angeles and Santa Fe.

Santa Anna returns from exile and prepares to regain presidency, August 12–18.

U.S. troops capture Monterrey, Mexico, September 20–24.

Californios reclaim Los Angeles area, September 30.

1847 U.S. troops reoccupy Los Angeles, January 10–19.

Santa Anna retreats to give victory at Buena Vista to United States, February 22–23.

U.S. troops attack Veracruz, March 26–29.

Santa Anna barely escapes at Battle of Cerro Gordo, April 18.

U.S. troops capture the Castle of Chapultepec.

U.S. troops begin occupation of Mexico City, September 13–14.

Santa Anna is overthrown and flees Mexico on October 7.

1848 Nicholas Trist begins formal peace negotiations on January 2.

Gold is discovered at Sutter's mill in California on January 24.

Treaty of Guadalupe Hidalgo is signed on February 2.

The United States formally ends occupation of Mexico on June 12.

1853 Santa Anna returns from exile and becomes president.

James Gadsden negotiates the purchase of additional land from Mexico by the United States.

GLOSSARY

amputate: to cut off a part of the body, usually an arm or leg, especially by surgery

annexation: adding a smaller territory to a larger one, such as the annexation of Texas to the United States

armistice: temporary end to fighting by a formal agreement of the warring armies

artillery: mounted guns or cannons that fire objects such as iron balls. Artillery may be light or heavy, depending on the size of the objects fired.

blockade: to shut off an area by use of enemy troops or ships to prevent the passage of supplies

campaign: a series of military operations or maneuvers

colony: a territory inhabited by people from a different country, but who retain ties with the parent state

dragoon: an army soldier who fights on horseback

dysentery: a disease of the intestine that causes bleeding and severe diarrhea

Manifest Destiny: an idea or doctrine, first stated in the 1840s, that it is the fate of the United States to dominate North America from the Atlantic to the Pacific

propaganda: the spreading of ideas, information, or rumor for the purpose of helping or injuring an institution, a cause, or a person

treaty: a formal agreement between two or more nations, signed and ratified (approved) by the governments of those nations

yellow fever: an infectious virus, carried by mosquitoes, that damages the liver and gives the skin a yellowish cast. Yellow fever is common in regions near the equator. Mosquito control has helped eliminate the disease in most urban areas. A vaccine developed in 1937 can also help prevent the spread of the virus.

WHO'S WHO?

Sarah Borginnis Bowman (ca. 1812–1863)

A nurse, cook, businesswoman, and soldier, Sarah Bowman—one of her many names—stood well over six feet. She was known as the Heroine of Fort Brown (Texas) because she cared for U.S. troops during the shelling there in May 1846. Bowman followed Taylor's campaign, marrying several soldiers along the way, while cooking, cleaning, and nursing the troops. She loaded cartridges and carried the wounded from the field at the Battle of Buena Vista. Known for her fearlessness and generosity (which included adopting several Mexican orphans), Bowman received a U.S. government pension for life and, after her death, was buried with full military honors.

John Frémont (1813–1890)

Known as the Pathfinder because of his mapmaking expeditions to Oregon and California, John Charles Frémont, born in Savannah, Georgia, started out as a mathematician with the U.S. Army Corps of Topographical Engineers. Bold and reckless, Frémont was court-martialed after a dispute over who held governing authority in California in 1846. He was nearly court-martialed for freeing the slaves of Missourians during the Civil War, when he served as commander of the Union (Northern) army's Western Department. Frémont grew rich during the California gold rush, became one of California's first senators, ran unsuccessfully for the presidency, and then lost all his money. Later, Frémont became governor of Arizona Territory.

Valentín Gómez Farías (1781–1857)

A middle-class Mexican doctor who gradually became involved in politics, Valentín Gómez Farías became convinced that rebellion was a legitimate way to bring democracy to newly independent Mexico. He supported a war to take back Texas and restore Mexico's 1824 constitution. Gómez Farías hoped joining with Santa Anna would help, but these plans failed when a revolt drove Gómez Farías's party from power. Gómez Farías then tried to hamper peace negotiations with the United States and rejected the Treaty of Guadalupe Hidalgo. When that also failed, Gómez Farías retired from politics.

Manuel de la Peña y Peña (1789–1850)

After he earned a law degree, Manuel de la Peña y Peña held several government positons when Mexico first gained independence. He later served as minister of foreign relations, minister of the interior, and justice of the Supreme Court. Peña y Peña first tried to prevent a war with the United States by encouraging government leaders to meet with special envoy John Slidell in 1845. When that failed, he helped to negotiate peace and supported the Treaty of Guadalupe Hidalgo as a way to end Mexico's suffering and bring about national stability. He died shortly after the war and was later recognized as one of Mexico's great leaders.

Samuel Ringgold (1800–1846)

The U.S. artillery corps was Samuel Ringgold's first assignment after graduating from West Point in 1818. Ringgold traveled to Britain and France to study artillery tactics and later revised the artillery manual for the U.S. Army. His flying artillery method allowed artillery pieces to be moved quickly and fired more accurately. Mortally wounded while directing artillery at the Battle of Palo Alto in May 8, 1846, Ringgold became a national hero.

Antonio López de Santa Anna (1794–1876)

A member of Mexico's upper-class elite, Santa Anna was a professional soldier who admired the French general and emperor Napoleon Bonaparte. Like Napoleon, he treated himself royally. Still, he managed to portray himself as a man of the people and a national hero. A wise politician, Santa Anna rose to power in the army and was the president several times over 20 years. During that time, Texas gained independence and Mexico lost half its territory in a war with the United States. Santa Anna sold even more land to the United States in the Gadsden Purchase.

Winfield Scott (1786–1866)

Born on a plantation near Petersburg, Virginia, Winfield Scott studied law, joined a volunteer cavalry unit, and then entered the U.S. Army in time to fight in the War of 1812. Gruff, efficient, and ambitious, Scott put his knowledge of military tactics to good use in the war with Mexico. The U.S. soldiers called him Old Fuss and Feathers because of his attention to detail and military etiquette. Scott ran for president in 1852 and lost to fellow officer Franklin Pierce. He ended his long military career after commanding Abraham Lincoln's bodyguards at Lincoln's inauguration.

Daniel Webster (1782–1852)

Thanks to the high value placed on education by his parents, who eked out a living on a farm in Salisbury, New Hampshire, Daniel Webster had private tutors by age four, graduated from Dartmouth College, and studied law. Webster made his mark on all three branches of government: as a congressman and senator; as secretary of state under Presidents Harrison, Tyler, and Fillmore; and as a lawyer arguing cases before the U.S. Supreme Court. Webster opposed annexation of Texas, war with Mexico, and slavery, but he argued strongly for the Compromise of 1850 (which allowed slavery in the South). He hoped the compromise would preserve the United States. Two years later, Webster was thrown from his horse and died.

SOURCE NOTES

5   Emory M. Thomas, *Robert E. Lee: A Biography* (New York: W. W. Norton & Company, 1995), 116.

9   Carol Christensen and Thomas Christensen, *The U.S.-Mexican War: Companion to the Public Television Series "The U.S.-Mexican War, 1846–1848"* (San Francisco: Bay Books, 1998), 19.

10   Christensen, 25.

10   Ibid., 47.

15   Margaret C. S. Christman, *1846: Portrait of a Nation* (Washington, D.C.: Smithsonian Institution Press, 1996), 5.

15   Linda S. Hudson, *Mistress of Manifest Destiny: A Biography of Jane McManus Storm Cazneau, 1807–1878* (Austin: Texas State Historical Association, 2001), 61.

15   Christensen, 53.

16   Ibid., 49.

19   Donald S. Frazier, ed., *The United States and Mexico at War* (New York: Simon & Schuster, 1998), 28.

20   Christman, 117.

21   Christensen, 62.

22   Ibid., 123.

23   "The Mexican-American War: 1846 to 1848," *A Shared Experience,* January 2, 2000, <http://www.rice.edu/armadillo/Past/Book/Part2/1846-8.html> (December 1, 2003).

23   Christensen, 69.

24   Samuel E. Morison and Henry S. Commager, *The Growth of the American Republic,* vol. 1 (New York: Oxford University Press, 1961), 590.

26   Christensen, 99.

27   J. D. Eisenhower, *So Far from God: The U.S. War with Mexico, 1846–1848* (New York: Random House, 1989), 214.

28   Christensen, 104.

29   Ibid., 111.

30   "Wilmot Proviso," *What You Need to Know About,* 2003, <http://americanhistory.about.com/library/blwilmotproviso.htm?terms=+wilmot+proviso> (December 17, 2003).

30   Ibid.

31   Pedro Santoni, *Mexicans at Arms: Puro Federalists and the Politics of War, 1845–1848* (Fort Worth: Texas Christian University Press, 1996), 133.

34   Thomas D. Tennery, *The Mexican War Diary of Thomas D. Tennery* (Norman: University of Oklahoma Press, 1970), 7.

35   Christensen, 132.

37   Tennery, 38.

38   Christensen, 149.

43   Ibid., 155.

43   Ibid.

43   Ibid., 154.

44   "Teaching With Documents Lesson Plan: Lincoln's Spot Resolutions," *U.S. National Archives and Record Administration,* n.d., <http://www.archives.gov/digital_classroom/lessons/lincoln_spot_resolutions/lincoln_spot_resolutions.html> (December 17, 2003).

44   Christman, 121.

44   Christensen, 192.

46   Ibid., 153.

46   Eisenhower, 247.

47   Hudson, 83.

48   Christman, 131.

49   Hudson, 84.

50   Anna Kasten Nelson, *Secret Agents: President Polk and the Search for Peace with Mexico* (New York: Garland Publishing, Inc., 1988), 79.

51   Hudson, 82.

51   Christensen, 171.

51   Nelson, 86.

52   Christensen, 135.

53   Gail Buckley, *American Patriots: The Story of Blacks in the Military from the Revolution to Desert Storm* (New York: Random House, Inc., 2001), 54.

54   Hudson, 84.

56   Christensen, 184.

57   Ibid., 186.

59   Mary C. Gillet, *The Army Medical Department, 1818–1865* (Washington, DC: Center of Military History, U.S. Army, 1987), 113.

60   Nelson, 83.

60   Christensen, 206.

61   Ibid., 59.

61   K. Jack Bauer, *The Mexican War: 1846–1848* (New York: Macmillan Publishing Co., Inc., 1974), 294.

61   Clifford Dowdey, *Lee* (Boston: Little, Brown and Company, 1965), 91.

61   Christensen, 69.

62   Ibid., 200

63   Ibid., 208.

65   Ibid., 214.

65   Ibid., 215–216.

65   Eisenhower, 365.

69   Ibid., 368.

69   Christensen, 219.

70   Ibid., 218.

70   Ibid.

70   Ibid.

73   Morison and Commager, 648.

76   "Chamizal National Monument," *National Park Service,* n.d., <http://www.nps.gov/cham> (December 17, 2003).

76   Tim Weiner, "Trying to Put Mexico First, with No U.S. in the Way," *New York Times,* January 26, 2003, 5.

SELECTED BIBLIOGRAPHY, FURTHER READING, AND WEBSITES

SELECTED BIBLIOGRAPHY

Bauer, K. Jack. *The Mexican War: 1846–1848.* New York: Macmillan Publishing Co., Inc., 1974.

Buckley, Gail. *American Patriots: The Story of Blacks in the Military from the Revolution to Desert Storm.* New York: Random House, Inc., 2001.

Caruso, A. Brooke. *The Mexican Spy Company: United States Covert Operations in Mexico, 1845–1848.* Jefferson, NC: McFarland & Company, Inc., 1991.

Christensen, Carol, and Thomas Christensen. *The U.S.-Mexican War: Companion to the Public Television Series "The U.S.-Mexican War, 1846–1848."* San Francisco: Bay Books, 1998.

Christman, Margaret C. S. *1846: Portrait of a Nation.* Washington, D.C.: Smithsonian Institution Press, 1996.

Dowdey, Clifford. *Lee.* Boston: Little, Brown and Company, 1965.

Eisenhower, J. D. *So Far from God: The U.S. War with Mexico, 1846–1848.* New York: Random House, 1989.

Frazier, Donald. S., ed. *The United States and Mexico at War.* New York: Simon & Schuster, 1998.

Gillett, Mary C. *The Army Medical Department, 1818–1865.* Washington, D.C.: Center of Military History, U.S. Army, 1987.

Hudson, Linda S. *Mistress of Manifest Destiny: A Biography of Jane McManus Storm Cazneau, 1807–1878.* Austin: Texas State Historical Association, 2001.

Nelson, Anna Kasten. *Secret Agents: President Polk and the Search for Peace with Mexico.* New York: Garland Publishing, Inc., 1988.

Nevins, Allan. *The Ordeal of the Union: Fruits of Manifest Destiny, 1847–1852.* Vol. 1. New York: Charles Scribner's Sons, 1947.

Santoni, Pedro. *Mexicans at Arms: Puro Federalists and the Politics of War, 1845–1848.* Fort Worth: Texas Christian University Press, 1996.

Tennery, Thomas D. *The Mexican War Diary of Thomas D. Tennery.* Norman: University of Oklahoma Press, 1970.

Thomas, Emory M. *Robert E. Lee: A Biography.* New York: W. W. Norton & Company, 1995.

FURTHER READING

Behrman, Carol H. *Andrew Jackson.* Minneapolis, MN: Lerner Publishing Company, 2003.

"The California Trail," *Cobblestone Magazine,* November 2002.

English, June A., and Thomas D. Jones. *Scholastic Encyclopedia of the United States at War.* New York: Scholastic, Inc., 1998.

Hamilton, Janice. *Mexico in Pictures.* Minneapolis, MN: Lerner Publishing Company, 2003.

Kent, Zachery. *Zachary Taylor: Twelfth President of the United States.* Chicago: Children's Press, 1988.

Marrin, Albert. *Empires Lost and Won: The Spanish Heritage in the Southwest.* New York: Atheneum, 1997.

Sullivan, George. *Alamo!* New York: Scholastic, Inc., 1997.

"The U.S.-Mexican War: 1846–1848," *Cobblestone Magazine,* December 2000.

WEBSITES

The Handbook of Texas Online <http://www.tsha.utexas.edu/handbook/online/> Information about the state and its history

"The Treaty of Guadalupe Hidalgo." *The Avalon Project at Yale Law School* <http://www.yale.edu/lawweb/avalon/diplomacy/mexico/guadhida.htm> The complete treaty online

"The U.S.-Mexican War." *PBSOnline* <http://www.pbs.org/kera/usmexicanwar/> Information connected with the PBS special about the Mexican-American War.

OTHER RESOURCES

The Chamizal National Memorial. The memorial, operated by the National Park Service, is located in El Paso, Texas, near the territory that the United States returned to Mexico in 1967. <www.nps.gov/cham>

Mexico: A Story of Courage and Conquest. Vol. 2, *From Independence to the Alamo.* Vol. 3, *Battle for North America.* New York: The History Channel, A&E Television Networks, 1999. These videotapes present information on Mexico from 1820 to about 1860, including the Alamo and the Mexican view of the Mexican-American War.

INDEX

ABOUT THE AUTHOR

Ruth Tenzer Feldman is an award-winning author, whose works include a biography of Thurgood Marshall, *How Congress Works, Don't Whistle in School: The History of America's Public Schools, World War I,* and *The Korean War.* A former attorney with the U.S. Department of Education, Ms. Feldman is also a frequent contributor to *Cobblestone* and *Odyssey* magazines. She shares her Bethesda, Maryland, home with her family, her Welsh corgi, and her trusty computer. She can be reached at RTFeldman@aol.com.

PHOTO ACKNOWLEDGMENTS

The images in this book are used with the permission of: Library of Congress, pp. 4–5 (LC-USZ62-62232), 6 (G3700 1839.B81 RR6), 17 (LC-USZ62-91388), 19 (LC-USZ62-1270), 20 (LC-USZ62-23836), 28 (LC-262-17905), 34 (LC-USZ62-3931), 35 (LC-USZ62-5327), 37 (LC-USZC2-2800), 41 top (LC-USZ62-109945), 41 bottom (LC-USZ62-102089), 44 (LC-USZ62-84833), 45 (LC-D418-8308), 48 (LC-USZ62-14216), 51 (LC-USZ62-5221), 55 (LC-USZ62-47990), 56 (LC-USZ62-62236), 61 (LC-USZC2-2939), 63 (LC-USZ62-62216), 65 (LC-DIG-cwpbh-02914), 74 left (LC-USZ62-5555), 82 (LC-USZ62-107503), 83 middle (LC-USZC2-3181), 83 bottom (LC-USZ62-11135); North Wind Picture Archive, pp. 7 top, 16 both, 24, 39, 46, 60, 75; © CORBIS, p. 7 bottom; Peter Newark's American Pictures, pp. 8, 9 both, 10, 18, 22, 25, 36, 42, 47, 50, 66, 71, 76; Independent Picture Service, p. 11; Denver Public Library, Western History Department, p. 15; Peter Newark's Pictures, pp. 23, 38; Peter Newark's Western Americana, p. 26; National Archives, War and Conflict Collection, pp. 27, 32, 33, 57, 62, 64, 67; Used by permission, Utah State Historical Society, all rights reserved, p. 30; painting by Paul L'Ourvier. Courtesy New York Historical Society, pp. 31, 83 top; Security Pacific Collection/Los Angeles Public Library, p. 69; The Huntington Library, San Marino, CA, p. 73; Texas State Library Archives Division, p. 74 right; © Bettmann/CORBIS, p. 77. Maps by Laura Westlund, pp. 12, 29, 40, 72, 79.

Cover image courtesy of the Library of Congress (LC-USZC2-2939).